D1523542

Dedication

I would first like to dedicate this book to my one and only healer, Jesus Christ, without whom there would be no light in my darkness.

Second, to my husband, Jason, and my boys, Michael and Hunter. You guys were my rocks, my laughter, my voice, and my heroes during every dark moment of this journey. I love you all more than words could ever express.

Table of Contents

1

Where it all Began

And the Lord sits as King forever.
The Lord will give strength to His people;
The Lord will bless His people with peace.
- PSALM 29:10b-11 (NKJV)

I really don't know where to begin. As I look back, I see nothing but the goodness of God in my life. I see His hand at work as He intricately wove a tapestry of freedom, love, and grace into every aspect of my life. In truth, my story is *His* story, and anything good, kind, or praiseworthy is from His gracious and merciful hands. Twenty years ago, my life was turned upside down with one news report, but before I go into that, let me give you a bit of my background.

A CHILD AFRAID

I grew up in a small town in Arkansas where even my birth was a miracle. At the time, my mother's doctor was on vacation, and when she began bleeding prematurely, the physician on duty told her I was dead. She was prepped for surgery but by the grace of God, her personal doctor came back early, and she told him she felt me move in the night. Sure enough, he checked, and I was not dead. From there, the delivery proceeded without incident, praise the Lord.

I was a very timid child, and the trauma I suffered in my first year of school only made it worse. My first-grade teacher's abusive behavior included throwing books at the students, as well as yelling and calling us names. Her standards were such that if we scored below a B, we would be punished. For instance, once she had her friend (who was also a teacher) dress up as a gorilla and come into the room and frighten us. We hid under our desks, scared out of our wits. I vividly recall the terror that rippled through my small frame as the "monster" approached. Because she warned us against telling our parents of these abusive incidents, I began to make up stomachaches or the like in order to miss school. This didn't always work, so I only grew more and more fearful.

All this time, my parents had no idea what was happening. They only knew I did not want to go, which they found surprising since when I attended kindergarten, I was up early every day, excited to "go to school." But now? Sometimes, my father was forced to chase me around the house as I cried, trying to avoid getting on the bus. Once, I even hid in the ditch when the bus came so I wouldn't have to go.

When I finally told them what was going on, they immediately demanded that the school withdraw me from that classroom. However, by this time, other students had already told their parents what was going on. The school decided they weren't moving anyone else, and they did not fire the teacher. As a result, I was prescribed nerve medication and spent the remainder of first grade visiting the counselor's office nearly every day.

Throughout my school years, I was bullied because I was so timid, and the kids knew they could easily make me cry. Our small town was all about social status, so I was shunned by some of the children because my parents weren't wealthy.

My parents loved me, but because of my mom's own trauma as a child, she did not understand what I was going through, nor how to help me. My dad worked long hours to keep food on the table so he could not be around as much as he (or we) would have liked.

Throughout my life, I struggled with anxiety and fear at varying levels. For instance, I was terrified of thunderstorms. I distinctly remember a time when a big one was brewing, I felt the safest place in the world was on my daddy's lap. My little heart raced as the lighting flashed outside our mobile home window. We only just recently endured a tornado that blew away our shed and in doing so, succeeded in cutting off our dog's tail. After that, every hint of rain sent me into anxiety that led to a paralyzing panic. Probably because of the danger mobile homes face in bad weather, Dad started making sure we left the house when the worst warnings were announced.

I was also dreadfully afraid of dying, constantly expecting to come down with cancer or some other disease that would kill me only after a long, drawn-out illness. I did suffer from bronchial asthma as a kid, and this made me sick a lot. One year, I spent two weeks in bed because I contracted pneumonia and stomach flu at the same time. I cried every day and repeatedly told my parents that I didn't want to die. They comforted me as best they could, but this morbid fear followed me into my adulthood.

A Bad Seed Takes Root

I'm twenty-four years old and watching a news report regarding the dangers of food allergies. This particular report concerned having peanuts in schools where children with severe allergies may come in contact and have an anaphylactic reaction.

I already had a bent toward being afraid to die, so my mind latched on to this news report like a dog on a bone. I was not taught to choose what we put into our minds and what we think about, so every time the fear of dying from a food allergy came to mind, I would research it online. It wasn't long before I learned that a person could be allergic to *any* food. I began avoiding the big ones like wheat, eggs, milk, peanuts, shellfish, and soy, but it wasn't long before that list grew to include almost every food. It got to where all I would eat was chicken, carrots, and broccoli. Within two months, I went from a proper 125 pounds to 108 pounds. The drop in weight was soon accompanied by severe panic attacks where my heart would race and flood my bloodstream with adrenaline.

Why Can't I Trust God?

I was scared all the time, yet also aware that I was supposed to depend on God for all things. Where was my faith, I'd ask inside, eventually filling with guilt because I couldn't trust God to take care of me. I would be on my face day after day crying out to God, trying to figure out what I could do to get Him to heal me. I read my Bible constantly and prayed all the time, but nothing seemed to help. I soon came to the conclusion that I was a bad Christian because I didn't have the faith required to get over my fear.

I continued to drop weight until finally my doctor told me that if I didn't eat, she would admit me to the hospital and feed me by a tube. The thought of being hospitalized and what all that entailed frightened me more than ever. When my doctor prescribed anxiety medicine, I began to eat a little better. But when slowly I began to see some healing, I went off the medication as soon as I could.

By now I had begun counseling sessions with a woman at our church. One day she told me, "Gina, the issue here isn't, *do you love God*. God knows you love Him. The issue is you don't know that God loves you." I thought about that a long time and still didn't know quite how to fix it.

My husband was in the military at this time, and we were transferred to a new base. I was doing better, but still cycled through bouts of anxiety and panic. Also, I remained very limited on what I would eat, still fearing a serious allergic reaction if I ate the wrong thing. On the outside, I worked hard to appear as an excellent Christian, but inside more than ever I struggled with trusting God.

The years passed and we moved again once my husband was out of the military. By this time, through counseling, I was learning about God's grace, how I can't *earn* anything from Him by my actions. At the same time, I was spinning my wheels trying to be good enough to earn His healing, trying to jump through the right hoops, pray the right prayers, and quote the right scriptures.

Throughout my childhood, I was taught that God was a harsh God and He punished us if we did not "walk the line." I was led to believe that if we wanted His healing, we had to live perfect, upright lives. The theme of my life had become, "I am not good enough, not smart enough, not rich enough, and not pretty enough." Because of that, I worked even harder to be good enough for God to heal me and use me in His kingdom.

From the time I was very small, singing with the other children before the congregation, I felt the pull of God on my life. I knew I loved God, and I wanted to live my life for Him.

As a teenager, even when I was not living my life for God, I still felt that pull, and would reason with God about whatever I was or wasn't doing right in His sight. I would pull out my Bible and pray He would forgive me, while at the same time, I went out the door, seeking a way to be good enough for someone to choose me to love.

Now here I was as an adult *still* trying to earn God's love, trying to be good enough for God to heal me and choose me. My heart was always to be in ministry. I loved praying for and ministering to people. It was in those times that I felt alive. I would try so hard to get God and the people around me to see that I was worth using in ministry. As I continued down this road, I absolutely wore myself out. In doing so, I weakened whatever measure of peace I had achieved, and my anxiety returned in force.

SETBACKS

By 2008, and I could no longer go to church because my panic attacks returned in force. I told myself that if I could just *change something*, I would get better. We moved several times, thinking a different location with different people would fix my problems. I ran up credit card debt thinking maybe if I dressed a certain way or had a certain house, people would like me and allow me to be in ministry. I tried everything I could think of, fasting, praying more earnestly and more frequently, reading my Bible more often. I cried out to God over and over, but none of that dampened my anxiety.

Eventually, I turned again to counseling which helped me return to the place of understanding. I admitted inside that I did not fully know God's love for me. The Bible says, *His perfect love casts out fear* (I John 4:18), yet I still felt I had to earn my healing. This was so ingrained that I could not let go of it. I could not try a new way because I worried, "what if the new way is wrong and I still never get healed?"

What if God was waiting for me to quote one more scripture out of the hundred I quoted all the time? What if God was waiting for me to pray one more prayer? Worship one more time? What if He responded and I somehow missed Him? What if I said the prayer a different way? Would that make it work? I loop these concerns in my head, constantly worrying that I was not doing something I should be doing, or doing something the wrong way, which prevented God from healing me.

I was told several times that I did not have enough faith, so I would try to *make* myself have faith. When that didn't work, I would fall apart one more time, more certain than ever that something was wrong with me.

Sometimes I doubted God heard my prayers. Then my mind would go to, *maybe God isn't even real.* If He was real, was He involved in my life? My husband likened this tendency of mine to a hamster on a wheel, constantly running.

I went through several years of this cycle, waking up every day with severe anxiety. Going through every hour, wondering if this would be the day I would die. Was there something wrong with my heart? Would I quit breathing? I made endless trips to doctors' offices, heart specialists, and allergists, sometimes spending hours in the ER, just to be told one more time that I was "only having a panic attack."

There came a time after the birth of my first child that upon hearing my symptoms, the doctor told me this very thing. "It's only anxiety and panic attacks." But it turned out to be

9

postpartum thyroiditis. The doctor apologized for his misdiagnosis and that condition resolved itself over time. But around this same time, I was diagnosed with a slight mitral valve prolapse.[1] This had my anxious mind scampering to investigate, where I latched onto the scariest case scenarios, adding one more possible dangerous medical condition to my worry list.

It was time to buckle down. I would *convince* God that I was worth healing. I would take my ministry more serious than ever, because as a minister to His people, I would be worth keeping alive, right?

In 2011, our family moved to Ozark, MO, again, mainly because I thought another move with new people would fix my problems. By this time, my boys and my husband were accustomed to my eating habits, picking my foods carefully and eating some more slowly. They were also accustomed to my cycles of anxiety and panic. In our new town, I started church counseling again because I *just knew* that would solve everything.

In 2012, we became youth leaders and even had a life group with the youth. Now I was *sure* God would heal me, because not only was I in church every Sunday and Wednesday night, but I was a youth leader. I think this idea came from churches we visited that taught if you weren't at church every time the doors

---

[1] Divine healing? In 2012, when tested again, my mitral valve prolapse had disappeared. It is our belief that God healed me of this diagnosis, bless His name!

were open, you weren't in God's will. In fact, one church gave us swipe cards to make sure we attended 75% of the time. I know now how ridiculous that sounds, but we were baby Christians and thought we were being told the truth. Oh, how the binds of legalism had already gotten their grip on me, doing their best to steal, kill, and destroy me utterly. Something had to be done before those binds literally choked out my life.

2

Fear is My Companion

Yea, though I walk through the valley of the shadow of death,
I will fear no evil; For You are with me;
Your rod and Your staff, they comfort me. —
PSALM 23:4 (NKJV)

In October 2013, things took a turn for the worst. This time it would take a while for me to get back on my feet. This time I truly believe I stared death in the face.

I tried to go to a women's conference at the church we were attending, once again believing that if I could make it there, I would find healing. God was sure to heal me if I just took this step of faith, or at least that is what I was being told.

So, I went. …And I panicked. My heart skipped beats and I just knew I was going to die. I had to leave, so once again, I felt like a failure as a Christian. Why was it that everyone else could have more faith and overcome the things they faced, and I was too weak to do the same?

After this, things went downhill, and I had to stop going to church again. I grew physically sick and couldn't eat. This time, though, the eating issue got even worse than before. I wasn't eating *anything* and was losing weight rapidly. I feared that at any moment, my heart would stop. From morning to night, it skipped beats. Evenings, sleep did not come easily, and I would wake up in the morning with severe leg cramps. Several nights while my heart was thumping and thudding, we ended up in the ER, to once again be told I had anxiety and panic attacks, and my heart was fine. I was low in magnesium and potassium, along with several other vitamins and minerals because of malnutrition, but eating made me frightened and very sick. I went from 125 pounds this time to 102 pounds within a couple of months.

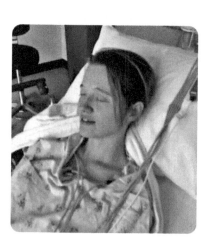

Me at 102 lbs., in the E.R. due to a panic attack.

Adrenaline again coursed through my veins all day and night, but this time it also made my heart beat erratically. I was sure at any point it would be my last breath. I could not leave my house and didn't want to be alone.

Luckily by this time, my husband was working from home for his job. Occasionally, he had to leave for business trips and my parents would stay with me. They said I looked like I was on death's door.

My clothes hung off my frame and I could not make it to the kitchen from the couch without my heart racing and feeling like I would pass out. I couldn't make it from my bed to the bathroom and often had to use the trashcan beside my bed as my toilet. I would look in the mirror and see this shell of a person who used to be there. I hated myself because I couldn't get better.

How had it gotten this bad, and most of all, where was God? I had done everything I was supposed to do. I had jumped through all the hoops. I had gone to church, and I had become a leader in the church. I constantly prayed and read my Bible. I lived a clean life, in fact, so much that most people thought I was a prude. I had done everything a good Christian should do and here I was close to death. Where was my God? Why had He abandoned me? As before, I would question was He even real, and if He was, why didn't He care that I was in so much pain and turmoil? And why wouldn't He take it all away?

Affecting My Marriage

Not only was I suffering, but my marriage was suffering. My husband didn't know how to handle what I was experiencing. He had to take care of our boys and do all the housework because I had no strength to do anything. I wrote a prayer request at a church during this time, and the lady emailed me back and told me I needed to stop being selfish and stop making my husband do all my chores. So many times during this period, it was reaching out to well-meaning Christians and getting answers like this that sent me further into a spiral of bondage and hating myself. It came to a point where I had to see my doctor and she recommended that my husband take me to the ER where they would evaluate me to see if I needed to go to a special facility. She said they wouldn't put me in the psych ward because I wasn't suicidal. Believe me, it wasn't for lack of having suicidal thoughts, but my biggest fear was death.

I figured by now that it wasn't God's fault; it was my fault. My faith was too weak, and I was such a failure. Once again, I wasn't good enough. I couldn't pick myself up by my bootstraps and be what God needed me to be. I was a failure as a wife and as a mother. Why wouldn't God just let me die? In my mind, that was what was going to happen. He would let me die so that my husband could enjoy life with someone else and my kids would have the mother they deserved.

So, we went to the ER to be evaluated. I remember this was one of the darkest days of my life. I cried and cried because I didn't understand how my family could bring me here and think about leaving me somewhere away from them. The room they put me in at the ER was very sterile and had been designed to house someone who was suicidal. There was only a cot-type thing. They made me take off everything and put on a gown and booties so there would be nothing I could hurt myself with. They brought me nerve medication and started doing an evaluation.

Afterward, they determined I was not bad enough to go to the psych ward, but I did need to go to a facility to get help. So, my husband and family drove me to this house that we had to tour. I just knew if they left me here, I would never see my family again because I would die. It was dark and drab, and I was crying and asking them to please not leave me.

I did not stay. We drove home and I promised everyone I would do better. I would do all the things I needed to do and have more faith, and I would get better. The doctor did convince me to start on anxiety medication. We tried four or five different medicines, and the side-effects were so bad that I would panic every time I had to take the pills. Eventually, I found a type that I could take one-fourth of the pill each time and did that until I could go off the pills entirely.

There would be days that I would cry all day. I remember my

dad sitting on the couch holding me and having tears in his eyes because he couldn't help. He and my mom were so scared I wouldn't live through it this time. I think I went through quite a few days that I didn't pray at all because, *why pray when no one was listening?* Or if they were listening, they didn't care. There were days when I didn't feel like I could take another breath, but somehow God gave me breath again.

My parents...

Slowly I began to be able to eat. I knew my husband was frustrated with me, and I was sure that he would walk out the door any day and never come back. I was at the point that the only people I could see without panicking were my husband and my kids. It was even hard to see my own parents, and I would have to take a pill right before they came. I would panic just trying to get into a car and go somewhere, and if my husband was out of my sight for long, I would freak out. He had his office in the basement, and I would go down there during the day to keep from being alone.

RESISTING BAD THOUGHTS

No one understood what was going on inside me. Everyone thought I could just control it somehow. They thought I just needed to make up my mind to be better and have more faith, and it would disappear. No one knew the thoughts of suicide that twirled around in my head, all the time knowing I wouldn't kill myself because I was so afraid of death. At the same time, I'd hear the voice of the enemy saying, *it is the only way out, and everyone will be better off when you are gone.*

I distinctly remember taking a shower one night later on in the battle, and I "saw myself" lying in the shower drenched in blood. I could feel darkness invading my entire being and whispering there was no other way. Only me and God truly knew the thoughts and fears that were a whirlwind in my head every moment of every day and every hour of the night.

I felt like I was worth nothing to anyone. I just *existed* for some reason, and God wouldn't let me die. There was one day I remember when my husband and I were sitting in the church parking lot waiting for my son to get out of a meeting, and my husband was frustrated with me because of something he wanted to do, but I didn't want him to do it because I didn't want to be left alone. He opened the car door and got out and said, "that's it, I can't do this anymore."

I started panicking because I just knew this was it; he was leaving me for good. I immediately took my one-fourth of a pill, knowing that taking that was going to cause side-effects and make me panic more. My husband got back into the car, and we headed home. I didn't dare tell him that my heart was racing and skipping beats and I was having trouble breathing, because I knew there would be no sympathy right now.

HEARING FROM GOD

As we drove home, I stared out the window and suddenly heard this: "When you walk through the fires of oppression, you will not be burned up; the flames will not consume you. You will walk out unharmed and unbound, not even smelling like smoke, better than you were before. My Word will not return to me void, but it will do what it was sent to do."

I knew I had heard it so clearly, yet at the same time, I questioned if it was God speaking. Later I told my husband about what I heard. A few days later, he listened to preaching on a podcast and told me that the preacher said exactly what I told him I heard. So, I listened to the podcast, and sure enough, it was the exact thing, word for word, even the exact translation God had used when I heard it. There is no way it could have been a coincidence, because this used three or four different scriptures simultaneously. Isaiah 43:2, "When you go through deep waters, I will be with you. When you go through rivers of difficulty, you will not drown. When you walk through the fire of oppression, you will not be burned up; the flames will not consume you." Daniel 3:25 & 27, "Look!" Nebuchadnezzar shouted. "I see four men, unbound, walking around in the fire unharmed! And the fourth looks like a god!" "Then the high officers, officials, governors, and advisers crowded around them and saw that the fire had not touched them. Not a hair on their heads was singed, and their clothing was not scorched. They didn't even smell of smoke!" and Isaiah 55:11, "It is the same with my word. I send it out, and it always produces fruit. It will accomplish all I want it to, and it will prosper everywhere I send it."

I held on to that word during the rough days and panic attacks ahead. I gradually began to eat some, get some strength, and get myself back up on my feet again. I was doing everything I knew to do in the natural and somehow still in my heart of hearts, holding on to hope that God would come through for me and that He was real, and He cared.

Another thing, I stopped doing everything that I was taught

by the church to do. God began speaking to me in my quiet time. I began to hear His voice in a way that I have never heard Him before. He began to sound like a loving Father instead of someone waiting to punish me and kill me at any moment. I was learning about rest, and this was when things began to turn for me. Hallelujah.

3

Finding Rest

Come to Me, all you who labor and are heavy laden,
and I will give you rest.
MATTHEW 11:28 (NKJV)

In 2015, God began showing me that my only way out of this was rest. I remember praying one night in my closet and God telling me that His love was enough to heal me and set me free. This is when I really began hearing God's voice in a new way. I began to see His true character.

The scripture that I would read over and over was Matthew 11:28-30 (TM), "Are you tired? Worn out? Burned out on religion? Come to me. Get away with me, and you'll recover your life. I'll show you how to take a real rest. Walk with me and work with me—watch how I do it. Learn the unforced rhythms of grace. I won't lay anything heavy or ill-fitting on you. Keep company with me, and you'll learn to live freely and lightly."

I began journaling the things that God was saying to me

more frequently than at any other time in my life. Throughout the remaining chapters of this book, I will share many of those writings with you, hoping that they will somehow help you and you will know that God is not a respecter of persons (Acts 10:34). He does not play favoritism. What God did for me, He will do for you. What He spoke to me, He will speak to you. It may not sound the same or look the same, but He will say exactly what you need.

Be Encouraged

I don't want this book to be a self-help book telling you a 12-step program, but I want it to be a guidepost, pointing you to God and His love and kindness. I want to encourage you to go to God in your situation and allow Him to speak to you and give you wisdom on what He wants you to do or not do. Let His voice be the ONE voice you listen to above all others because only He truly knows what is best for you. For me, God was saying *rest*. It was contradictory to what everyone else around me, including people in the church, were telling me to do. In fact, when I told one lady that God wanted me to rest, she told me I was just lazy! Again, a lot of the hurt I experienced during this time came from inside the church walls. I was told I was stubborn and just didn't want to do what others told me to do. Ultimately, I had to learn to listen to God, no matter who told me something else.

I wrote this in my journal:

Don't follow someone blindly or do what they tell you to do just because they are a pastor or may seem more spiritual than you. Take it to God, ask Him what to do, and see if it matches. If not, go with God's direction. Every man makes mistakes and gets it wrong sometimes. God's ways are always right and perfect.

I can tell you that if I had listened to man instead of God, I would probably either be dead from exhaustion right now or really close to it. God was saying to me, *rest*. He told me, "Stop it, Gina. Stop struggling and striving and trying to earn everything from me. You are wearing yourself out trying to get me to give you something you already have, My love and affection. You cannot earn my blessings. Everything you need was already paid for at the cross of My Son, Jesus. He did everything that needs to be done. There is nothing you can add to what He did, and when you try, it is like saying what He did was not enough. He purchased your freedom, your healing, everything you will ever need. I love you so much that I did not even spare my own Son. Do you really think there is anything I would not do for you if I knew it was what was best for you? Trust me. Let go and rest."

25

LEARNING HOW GOD DEFINES REST

Rest? What even did rest mean or look like? I was like, okay God, you want me to rest, but isn't that what I have been doing for almost three years now, resting? I have been stuck on the couch and in my bed, hardly able to do anything. I have done nothing but rest. But the *rest* God was speaking of was more than physical rest; it included that, but more than that, it was mental, emotional, and spiritual rest.

Even God rested from His work. The Bible talks about in Hebrew 3:19 how many would not enter rest because of unbelief. He began to show me that unbelief was the belief that He had not done everything that needed to be done, and so we work in turmoil trying to earn what he already died to give us.

I heard His voice as a Father talking to a daughter instead of a dictator talking to a servant. Over and over, He would whisper rest. I did things in the natural to try to help my body. I tried yoga and different meditation practices, none of which included any kind of Eastern religion. I always focused it on Jesus. In the end, I found the best thing for me was to just breathe in His presence. Just sit with Him. There wasn't any need to speak or try to pray. Just breathe deeply and sit with my Father.

As I found more healing, I began to pray again, but even my prayers had changed by this time. I was brutally honest with God. Pouring out my heart to Him and telling Him exactly how I felt, instead of trying to say the right words in the proper order or have enough faith. I allowed myself to feel the emotions that I felt and talk through them with my Father. I felt more and more freedom. I read my Bible less, but God showed me I was reading it for the wrong motives anyway. I was no longer trying to watch Christian television all hours of the day or listen to Christian music all the time. I allowed myself to enjoy life with my family.

Of course, there were boundaries with television and music, but God began to show me it was okay to enjoy life and that He was glorified when we are full of joy and fully alive. He is the creator of everything good, and just because it doesn't have the label of "Christian" on it doesn't mean God isn't in it or can't use it. He gives us our likes and dislikes, and it is okay to have them and enjoy them. Again, I am in no way advocating crossing boundaries that would be into sin but allow yourself to live. I wasn't living. I was so bound up all the time trying to make God pleased with me and trying to please everyone around me. I walked on eggshells in my relationship with God, so afraid at any moment, He would allow something bad to happen to me if I made a mistake or a bad decision. I didn't know about grace at all. I know now that it is finished, and it is all about Him. There is nothing I can do to make Him love me more or less. Jesus finished the work at the cross. It has everything to do with Him!

GROWING MORE HOPEFUL

By 2016, my body had healed tremendously, and I was on my way to what I believed was complete freedom. I still couldn't go to church, but I know now there was a reason that church was one of the last things I could do. God did not want me to be around all the other voices and trying to please those voices. He wanted me to hear His voice. I could go shopping and be around more family members, and I was eating again—almost anything I wanted to eat. I heard God say that He would use my story to be a beacon of light for others around me, those who were watching, and those I didn't even know yet.

God showed me He was and always had been in complete control of this battle and that at every moment, He was controlling everything. He only allowed the enemy so much rope, and His hands of protection had never left me. I could see His hand on my life at every single turn. I was never out of His sight or forgotten, even though it felt like it. He was always there beside me, and every time I felt like I couldn't go on, He would give me strength.

Every time I felt like I couldn't take another breath, He would make me breathe. He was always there, even when I couldn't see Him or feel Him, and He was never mad at me, even when I doubted that He even existed. He was okay with my emotions and my doubts because He knew the end of the story.

So, Here We Are.

I am healing, and the fear is subsiding. The anxiety is dwindling, and my body is stronger. Even the food issues seemed to be resolving, and then March 2017 came. The following are a few of my journal entries from this time.

January 31, 2015

I don't want to die. I just don't want to die. I don't want to have to take medicine, but I don't want to die either. I am so scared right now. I hate having these heart palpitations. I absolutely hate them. Why can't this be all over with? Why can't God just heal me now?

February 2015

It's always the same thing- nothing is changing, nothing is going to change. You still can't eat. You still can't go anywhere. You still have panic attacks, you still can't handle conflict, you still have heart palpitations. Nothing has changed, and it will never change. You are going to be like this for the rest of your life. You will have to force yourself to do these things, and because you cannot do that, it is hopeless...

THE DEVIL IS A LIAR, and there is NO TRUTH in him!!!

April 8, 2016

Saw a picture of an eagle soaring effortlessly over the mountains. God was saying to me the eagle doesn't fight with the mountain. It doesn't go around the mountain. It doesn't even climb the mountain. It just spreads its wings and rises over the mountain. I don't want you to stand there and fight this mountain. I want you to let go, spread your wings, and rise over this mountain.

Soar= maintain altitude without moving the wings or using an engine, effortless.

An eagle rest, trusting the wind to carry it. It doesn't even need to flap its wings. This is not a battle that you are to fight. You are to rest and let me fight for you. Let me be your Hero. Rest=Trust. In trust exercises, someone surrenders and falls back into the arms of the person they are trusting. I want you to fall back into my arms. I can carry the load. I can handle the weight of it. I will carry you, just like the wind carries the eagle. It is not work on the eagle's part. It just lets go. Trust me to do this. I will not fail you. I will not drop you. Resting is trusting me with every detail, knowing my way is perfect.

Trusting even when your eyes don't see, and your emotions don't agree. Resting is active. Trusting is active. It is a posture that you take on the inside. It is the position of your heart. Don't fight it, just rest...trust.

You cannot rest if you are not trusting because you will always try to figure it out. Trying to fix it in your own efforts. You will always try to fight the mountain or figure out a way around it or a path to climb it.

Isaiah 66:9

Would I ever bring this nation to the point of birth and not deliver it? No! I would never keep this nation from being born," says your God.

God did not bring me to this point just to let me down. He will bring this all the way through to completion.

4

Here We Go Again

My God, My God, why have You forsaken Me?
Why are You so far from helping Me,
And from the words of My groaning?
PSALM 22:1 (NKJV)

In March 2017, I caught a virus that took me a month to recover from. I thought I was healed and on my way back to health when suddenly, my body crashed. I lost all energy and started having severe palpitations and anxiety. I could barely make it to my bedroom from the living room, and once again, my husband had to take over the household chores.

What happened? I researched everything I could to figure out why my body crashed as it did after this virus. I now believe there were a couple of things going on. One, I was dealing with a histamine intolerance, which an allergist has since confirmed. And two, I was pushing myself so much to get better that my adrenal glands became fatigued. At the time, though, all I could think was that it had something to do with the food I was eating. My solution? Stop eating almost everything.

I was devastated. Hadn't I finally been on the road to complete freedom? How could God let this happen? How could He possibly give me freedom and then snatch it back again? I did not understand and fell into the same pattern, falling even deeper into depression because I had truly believed this was about to be over. I had been headed for the mountain top, but instead, I fell back into a valley deeper than before.

During this time, I went through many dark days and nights, and wrote the following in my journal, as well as posted it on Facebook and Instagram:

Fear is a prison that I can't break out of. Fear is a creature with its tentacles wrapped around me, and I can't get free. I can see freedom. I can taste freedom but never quite obtain it. I am scared to live and scared to die. It hurts to pray. It hurts to believe. It hurts to expect and never receive. Fear is a dark dungeon where there is no light. Who will come and rescue me from these chains? Where is my Savior? I know He hears me calling, but why won't He come? Where is He? Does He really care? Is He really there? Where is the light? Why won't it invade the darkness? I sit here in my dungeon alone. Who will come and rescue me? I can see the window. I can see freedom in my mind. I can even taste its sweetness, but yet it seems nowhere near. It eludes me. Fear laughs at me. It tells me I belong to it forever, that there is no way out. That my life is doomed to this dungeon. Yet something or someone deep inside still hopes, still believes, still cries out for my Savior to rescue me and set me completely free. Where is my Savior? Why has He left me here? When will He come?"

It seemed that I had completely lost hope this time. I got to the point that I would no longer allow myself to expect healing and freedom. It simply hurt too much to hope, to get excited or expect something good, just to turn around and be disappointed again. I wouldn't allow myself to go there.

I went through the motions of prayer trying to find a good place with God again, but it was just too hard. I went through much of each day in depression and a daze. I didn't reach out to many people because I didn't want to hear another "Christian" answer. I was tired; I thought I had done everything I was supposed to do. I thought I was resting, but still, here I was back in the same pit, and it looked like there would never be a way out.

Now and then, I would have moments of clarity, but they were few and far between. And when I thought I heard God speak, I would immediately doubt that it was Him and convince myself that I made it all up.

I returned to doctors, seeking answers in the natural, but got nothing. I was pretty sure at this point, that this was it for the rest of my life. I endured at this rate for two years until one day, I told my husband, *I can't do this anymore. Either I need help, or I'm not going to make it.* By this time, I was having serious thoughts of suicide because I just couldn't find a way out. I told my husband that I didn't want to be one of those people who got so far into depression and discouragement and never got help that finally took care of the situation themselves.

I didn't *want* to need help because I thought that meant I was a failure and a bad Christian. I wanted to do this on my own with just God's help, but that was not His plan. I realized later that getting help took more strength and courage than trying to do this alone.

January 28, 2017

HELP ME BELIEVE!!!

February 18, 2017

I have tasted fear's bitter pill. Oh, how bitter it is. Now I have tasted God's pure love, I can see the light again. There is hope, joy, and expectancy. How sweet it is! How sweet it is! I have never known a love as pure as His. For it was not my faith that broke my chains and drove out the darkness of fear. It was God's love that made my sight so clear. How sweet it is! How sweet it is to know love as pure as His.

May 13, 2018

Jesus, will I ever be free? Please tell me what to do. Please, Lord, help me! I do not want to live like this for the rest of my life. It feels like you are really silent right now. Where are you? I need to know what to do. Please help me! Are you hearing me? Please answer me!

October 2018

Anxiety hurts. It hurts you and everyone around you. Somehow people think you can just snap out of it. Just trust God. Just believe your way out. It doesn't work like that. Severe anxiety takes over your whole life and mind, and trying to read and confess scriptures about anxiety can just make it worse. There is a difference between someone who has anxiety about one or two situations and someone who lives every day riddled by anxiety. It has nothing to do with a lack of faith. It is a storm in your life, and people telling you to just trust God or believe more or have more faith only makes you feel worse. It brings more guilt and condemnation. Well-meaning people who try to help you only harm you by telling you to trust God and push through.

October 18, 2018

"Lean into Me. Put all the weight on Me. Let Me carry the load. Let Me carry you. I just want you to rest. Let your mind and your body rest. Don't try to be in control of everything and everyone else's lives. I've got you, and I've got them. I will take care of it all.

Allow Me to heal you and stop worrying about everything. Let Me speak to you. I want to do a work in you, then out of the overflow of that work will be your ministry. I want you to share what I speak, but first, take it in for yourself. Go back and read what you have shared with others, and don't read it as if I was giving it to you just to pass along, but as if it was specifically for you as well. Before you can help others, you have to heal. You can't keep trying to help others while you are still not healed; you won't last. You will crumble. Let go of what is ahead and let Me heal you now. Let Me take care of you now. It will have so much more meaning and impact."

October 2018

I feel like God is saying that I am in the healing process. In the healing process after major surgery or sickness, you have to rest. You have to guard against others bringing viruses and infections into your home. Rest is such an important part of the healing process. I also feel like God is asking me to silence all other voices trying to tell me who I am and allow Him to whisper who I am. In the healing process, I have to allow Him to take care of me.

He wants me in this time to draw close to Him alone and lean into His voice. Exactly what I have been telling everyone else to do. He was speaking those things to me also. Watch what happens when you let go and fall completely into your Father's arms and just allow Him to heal you!

October 21, 2018

"Baby girl, keep your eyes focused on Me. Don't be in a hurry. I will do more than you can imagine. Remember what you said to others about the butterfly? Don't rush the process. Let me develop you and strengthen your wings, and baby, when you are ready, you will fly. You will dance, you will leap, you will run, and I will restore the joy of a child to you."

Joy - I want it again. I want to live again. I want to be free from fear like I have never been before. Free to dance and live life to the fullest. Letting my heart sing to you. I want to fall in love with God and His Word.

5

Help is on the Way

Where there is no counsel, the people fall;
But in the multitude of counselors there is safety.
PROVERBS 11:14 (NKJV)

In March 2019, I began the search for a Christian counselor. I prayed God would lead me to the right person and He absolutely did. This person showed me things through counseling that I did not even realize I was dealing with. I discovered deep past traumas that I had not dealt with and allowed God to heal. I wasn't receiving my healing because I wasn't looking past the fear and anxiety to the root of the problem.

The biggest thing for me was my view of God and my view of myself. God spoke to me about *wounds*. Healing our emotional wounds is like healing our physical wounds. I get discouraged because it is taking so much time to heal. I felt God said to trust the process. He gave me the picture of a mom trying to pull a splinter out of a child's finger. She can't get it out if the child doesn't sit still and allow her to pull it out. And the wound can't begin healing if the splinter isn't removed. *The wound heals from the inside out.* There is a process! When I researched "wound healing," here are a few things that stuck out:

- Even though there is a general process, not everyone heals the same. Each individual is unique. There is no one size fits all approach.

- Healing is dictated by the depth of the wound. Superficial wounds only reach the first layer of skin and heal quickly. Deeper wounds extend further, and more has to happen for healing.

- Wounds always heal from the inside out. There can be many uncomfortable symptoms while the wound is healing, but those are signs that healing is happening.

- Almost every deep wound forms a scar where the skin at that location will not be as strong as the rest.

- It is essential to keep the wound covered and safe during the healing process.

It is amazing how well each of those parallel emotional and spiritual healing. In the healing of a wound, you must clean out whatever debris is present, be it dirt, gravel, splinters, glass, etc. No matter how much medicine you apply, the wound will not heal until those things are out. Once those things are cleared away, the medicine can penetrate and heal the wound.

The realization? God's love and healing could not penetrate my wounds because they had not been thoroughly cleaned out. I had been trying to slap medicine over the wound and cover it with a Band-aid, thinking that was all I needed to do. My solution was to begin with my counselor, cleaning out my wounds.

At first, the counseling caused more anxiety than it helped. The sessions were intended to be online with video, but I couldn't do the video because it made me too nervous. We were able to proceed by doing the sessions audio-only. I am so thankful for a kind and compassionate counselor who did not make me feel like I was a failure. We worked through wounds that I didn't realize I still carried from childhood to the present.

Again, I encourage you if you need help, get it; do not try to walk through it on your own. It takes a very strong person to seek help. It does not mean you are weak, rather, it means you are quite courageous. Asking for help and allowing someone else into your private world (and being honest with them during the process) takes bravery. In the end, it will absolutely be worth it.

FIXING THE SKEW

As I said, the biggest thing I found out was that I had been taught a very skewed view of God and of myself. I believed God was hard and harsh and wanted to punish me, and there were certain things I had to do to earn His approval and appease Him. I also believed that I was a failure, that everything I was going through was my fault, and that I was not good enough for anyone, let alone a holy and perfect God. I wish I could explain to you the weight lifted off me when I was told the truth of Who God is and who I am in Him, and how much He loves me. For the first time, not only was I told these things, but I *believed* these things, and I saw that what I was going through was not a punishment from God for things I had done. In fact, I wrote this on my phone:

"This is not a punishment from God; this is not judgment or consequences. This is an attack from the enemy on my life and mind. He has come to steal, kill and destroy, but it will not work. He does not get to win. He does not get to write my story. God has already written my story, and this is not the plan He has for me. This is not the end of my story. God has so much more beyond this. My life is not over, and God is not mad at me because I am struggling with this. This is not my battle. God has got this one, and all I need to do is stand still and see His deliverance. The fears I have seen today I will never see again. God loves me extravagantly, and His love is unconditional and unshakable, and unwavering. It is not over."

It makes a big difference when guilt and condemnation are removed from a situation you have blamed yourself for. You begin to see that the decisions you have made in your life were influenced by traumas that you have endured and subsequently survived. Though it is up to you to *decide* to change, you cannot change what you do not know about. This is why I encourage you to speak with someone to help you understand why you have made certain decisions that have hurt or sabotaged you, and why none of this is evidence of God punishing you.

We cannot control the environment we grow up in as kids. From a young age, we develop pathways in our brains, much like a series of roads. Every time those decisions are made for you and you are put through trauma, it wears that pathway more and more. You have to first recognize the trauma before you can begin to plow new pathways in your brain. Until then, every decision you make, every reaction you have, will flow through the filter of those pathways formed by trauma.

This is not something you can do overnight, but slowly and

surely, and with God's help, you can create new paths. It means changing the way you see God and how you see yourself. Allow yourself to begin to speak and believe the truth of who God says you are. To begin to believe that you are completely and totally loved, and that you are worth Him sacrificing His most precious possession for, His Son.

Again, these pathways were not created in one day, and you can't create new ones in one day, but as you begin to plow new ones, the old ones will begin to heal. You cannot heal from trauma on your own. Allow others you can trust to step into the process with you. Those who will encourage you and strengthen you, not tear you down and thus, hurt the process. Ask God who those people should be.

Also, you cannot heal from the trauma if you do not remove yourself from it and set boundaries for those who have caused it. It is like trying to bandage your wounds while you are still being fired upon. This may mean you have to completely cut people out of your life, either for a short time or for good, but you are worth healing.

This is a time when you must guard yourself against a myriad of different voices bringing contradictory advice. Ask God before you allow someone to speak into your life. Think about it. When you are sick, you don't want others bringing different viruses and germs into your home. My counselor said, *treat it like you are in the ICU.* When you are in the ICU, only certain people are allowed in, and you are very protected. You cannot help anyone else out of the trenches if your own wounds prevent you from getting out yourself.

Counseling and wound healing are emotional. It will bring up some strong feelings, but make sure you have a compassionate and trustworthy counselor to help you. Also, make sure you involve God in the process; only God can truly heal you completely and deeply. Only God can lead and guide you and your counselor to what you need for healing. If at any time you feel you are being told to do something that you do not feel comfortable with or feel is outside of God's will, speak up and let your counselor know. This could mean you have to change counselors. I had to do that a couple of times in this process. Whatever you do, don't give up.

One of my main motivations for seeking counseling was my family. My son was getting married. I wanted to be there at his wedding, so I knew I had to get help. I simply could not let my family down one more time. There was a lot of guilt and shame that I had to deal with in my counseling.

I felt shameful as a Christian that I "didn't trust God enough" to be healed.

I felt ashamed of my past.

I felt shameful for making my husband and kids suffer.

So much shame whirled around in my mind all the time. Praise the Lord, this is one of the things that God absolutely set me free from.

LEARNING THAT IT'S NOT MY FAULT

My counselor helped me see that the things I was dealing with were not my fault, and my family loves me enough to go through this battle with me. I was not causing this on purpose, nor was I trying to hurt anyone on purpose, and if someone could not understand, it was on them, not me. God understood where I was and why I was in that place. He understood that I needed help and that I could not get through this alone; in fact, He didn't want me to. Swallowing my pride and asking for help was one of the steps that God had me take on this journey. It was hard sharing my innermost things with someone else, but that was the only way to truly receive deep healing to the deep wounds. God was gracious to take me through it slowly and give me a counselor who would guide me with compassion and understanding, never judging or condemning me if I needed to stop or slow down.

Do not let shame stop you from receiving your healing. Shame is a liar. You and I are handpicked by God and chosen for a purpose and a plan. Psalms 34:5 in the NLT says, "Those who look to Him for help will be radiant with joy; no shadow of shame will darken their faces." Looking to Him for help looked like working with a counselor, but it may look different for you. Just continue to go back to the Father and ask what His plan is for you for your healing. He loves you so much, and He wants to help you. He wants to heal you. You are His chosen instrument. His prized possession. The apple of His eye. Allow Him to pour His love and healing balm out on you, how ever that looks for you.

Just continue to seek His face, and He will answer, I promise. It may not look the way you want it to, and the answer you get may not be what you want to hear, it wasn't for me, but He knows what is absolutely perfect and best for you, so trust His way. Psalms 18:30 says, "His ways are perfect, and all His promises prove true." He will not ever tell you to do something that will hurt you. It may hurt at first because cleaning out a wound hurts, but it will get better and better.

Finally, I was beginning to understand my worth, and that God was not mad at me. That He was actually very much in love with me. His love for me is extravagant. It is not cautious. Ephesians 5:2 in the TM says, "Watch what God does, and then you do it, like children who learn proper behavior from their parents. Mostly what God does is love you. Keep company with him and learn a life of love. Observe how Christ loved us. His love was not cautious but extravagant. He didn't love to get something from us but to give everything of himself to us. Love like that."

I began to speak to God through relationship instead of obligation. I actually could tell that I was believing what He says about me instead of what life and people had told me I was. My body slowly began to heal. I still was hesitant to expect healing or hope too much for it because of how things had gone in the past, but I slowly allowed myself to expect and hope a little more.

With all that, though, I still was dealing with one major issue; I was still in bondage to *legalism*. Such as being afraid that God might not heal me if I didn't do certain things, like read my Bible, or watch Christian television, or listen to only Christian music. I was afraid that God would never heal me completely because I wasn't in church. Thankfully, in His mercy, God began to deliver me from this as well. He began to show me it is okay to enjoy life, and He even spoke to me in times that I was not doing something "spiritual." I'm not advocating not reading your Bible or listening to Christian music, but when you are doing it for the wrong motives, maybe you should step away from it for a time. I did, and my counselor encouraged me to. I needed the things I was doing to become part of intimacy with God, part of a relationship. Not something I was doing to appease God or get Him to heal me.

My Faith Grows

The Word of God is not a magic wand, and there is no formula you can use or magic potion you can take to get God's blessings or answer to your prayers. The purpose of God's Word is to point us to His love and to His Son, Jesus Christ. God encourages us through Scripture, speaks to us through it, and through it, builds our faith in Him.

Faith. That word has been so hard for me. I was taught faith meant that I would do all these things, and God would answer my prayers. Or if I believed harder that it would be done, God would do it. Faith in the New Testament is actually just trust. My faith or trust is not in my own ability to believe, but my faith is in what Jesus did at the Cross. He said, "It is finished." *He* is the object of my faith. I behold the Cross. I begin to understand that cross represents the Father's love for me and that He conquered it all for me. I can rest in that.

Faith is a fight to believe that Jesus has finished it all. It has nothing to do with me and everything to do with Him. I trust that the Father loves me. He loves me so much that He did not even spare His own Son. Colossians 2:15 says, *"He stripped the powers of darkness of their power and made a spectacle of them on the Cross."*

IT IS FINISHED!

My salvation, my healing, my freedom, it has all been paid for and finished. Not by something I did or can do, but because of what Jesus did for me. If you or I had been the only ones on the earth, He still would have done it.

Through all of this, my heart was towards God. Even through the questioning and the doubt. I always knew that if God didn't come through, there was no hope. So even though I may have felt hopeless at times, in the depths of my heart, there was always at least a small sliver of hope. I encourage you to spend time with God every day. Even if all that looks like is sitting quietly not saying a word or even if you sometimes end up yelling at God; He can take it. If all you can say is, *Jesus help me,* or, *where are you, God?* That is having your heart toward Him.

God gave me a picture of myself underwater. I had a harness-type thing on my shoulders fixed with chains. Attached to the chains was a cinder block. It was holding me under the water, and every once in a while, I would be able to get to the surface and take a breath, but then it would pull me right back under. Then suddenly, the chains burst, and I swam to the top and away from it. I walked to the edge of the water and looked out and saw it disappear for good. I turned and walked away with a smile on my face and joy in my heart.

God spoke to me explaining that this was *legalism.* The chains of this breaking were the final step in my freedom. It spoke of the battle I had been in and how I would get freedom for a little while, and then it would pull me right back under. How it was exhausting me as I would try to free myself and try to figure out how to get loose on my own. All the trying to swim and flailing to get free only served to keep me exhausted. The moment I stopped trying to do it on my own and instead, simply rested in His finished work, I allowed God to break the chains, making me free for good. God took me to Ephesians 5:1 in the TM, "Christ has set us free to live a free life. So take your stand! Never again let anyone put a harness of slavery on you." In December 2019, I was able to see my brother for the first time in 6 years. It was such a great day. I hugged him so hard that day. What a great way to end the year!

July 8, 2019

Jesus asked for a different way, but He chose to trust the process of the way God was choosing to do things. What if Jesus would have given up? But He chose to trust God and changed history forever, and opened up access to the Father for us. I think for me, God is saying again, trust the process. I wanted Him to just do a miracle and take this away. I didn't want to have to go through counseling, but for some reason, this is the way He has chosen for my healing. But if I trust the process, what is on the other side will be so much more amazing than if he had just taken this away.

August 8, 2019

God loves me. He is not mad at me. He has been guiding me all along the way. Not one moment has been out of His reach or control. He has seen and known every step. Every step has a purpose. He is leading, guiding, and helping me navigate. It seems like He hasn't been listening or moving, but He has been working all along. It is His timeline, not mine. His ways, not mine. He sees the big picture. He knows what is best. He knows what is ahead. He wants me completely free.

It is and has been a long process, but He wants it to be a complete work and has led me along the right step at the right time. He has always had the big picture in mind.

The picture of my husband and my sons and leading and guiding them along their paths. It all fits together as one complete piece. It isn't just an individual picture; there are more players involved than just me. There are so many other lives entwined with mine. He intricately navigates each thread of each life together as a whole.

There is purpose in His work. Purpose that I can't even begin to see or fathom yet, but it is there. Meaning to each step and the timing of each step. He is the navigator; all I have to do is trust Him. Trust His goodness and His ways, Trust His love for me. He will get me where I need to be. Even though the journey seems so long and I don't always understand, in the end, when I look back, I will see it was all worth it. I will see all the pieces fitting together perfectly and the clear picture of the beauty and extravagance He was creating all along the way. Each step has a purpose that right now only He knows. Keep trusting. Keep moving forward. I will get there."

August 23, 2019

God sees me through the lens of the blood of Jesus. He sees me today, right now, as righteous, holy, and blameless without a single fault, not because of what I have done or can do, but because of the blood of Jesus.

When He sees me, He does not see the mistakes or poor decisions. I have done the best I could each step with what I had. He just sees His pure and spotless daughter, and He is well pleased with me. His heart is just to heal the pain and see me experience His love and freedom. He sees who He made me to be. He placed everything in me to equip me to become that.

I need to remind myself over and over that how He sees me is truth. I will know the Truth, and the Truth will see me free. Whom the Son sets free is free indeed. I think about it and realize that the person God has called me to be, has always already been inside of me. The potential to become that person is there.

The enemy has been very good at whispering lies throughout my life in various ways to keep me from realizing and experiencing that person. To keep me believing I am not worth loving or protecting, and that I am not good enough, that God is not pleased with me.

When I realize the truth, I will step into being the person God created me to be, and it will bring glory to God, and lives around me will be changed. This is not who God created me to be. He did not create me to be anxious and scared, and isolated all the time. He created me to shine for Him. To know I am loved and share that love with others. He created me for relationship with Him and to trust HIs goodness. Trust that His intentions toward me are good. He created me to thrive, to be beautiful, and to be His daughter. To feel protected and safe.

I am a daughter of the King. A king's daughter knows who her daddy is, and that gives her confidence. I was created to shine! It is okay to be proud of myself and know I am precious and valuable. It is ok to carry myself with worth and confidence, to hold my head high. That's how He created me."

I saw God come over to me and wipe my tears. I could hear Him say to me, "This is not your fault. I am not mad at you, I love you, and I am proud of you. I am not punishing you; I want to heal you and make you whole. I have good intentions for you. Will you allow me to heal you? Will you trust that I know what is best for you? Will you trust My timing and My ways are perfect? Will you take My hand and allow Me to lead you through this fire without trying to earn it or striving for it, or trying to help Me fix it?

Will you surrender it to Me? When you get through this fire, you will see the only thing that has been burned were the chains that bound you. You will look back and actually be thankful for the fire."

The scripture that came to my mind was Jeremiah 29:11 in the TM, "I know what I'm doing. I have it all planned out, plans to take care of you, not abandon you, plans to give you the future you hope for."

I think about that last part and the future I have told God I hope for. A future without being limited and paralyzed by fear but living free and unbound and being His vessel. To know what it is like to really experience life.

October 10, 2019

God is beyond my capacity to believe, imagine, understand, or comprehend. He is so much greater. What I can dream or ask or envision for my life, He is beyond that. My mind has limitations and boundaries to what I can dream or imagine, but He doesn't. He is beyond those things. He is beyond the beyond. I could never comprehend or fully ask or imagine what He has for me. He is so much greater than my limitations.

It makes me think of Ephesians 3:20:
"Now to Him who is able to do far more abundantly beyond all that we ask or think, according to the power that works within us," Ephesians 3:20 NASB

October 19, 2019

I sit here in my quiet room. In my journal, I wrote that I have cried out to God to heal my body and the eating situation many times. I just feel like I am fooling myself by having hope that God will heal me and set me free completely and use my life. I can't do this anymore.

I think I am just seeing and hearing what I want to see and hear. Maybe it is time for me to just face the reality that this is my life, go to the doctor to let them put me on medication. Just face that I will be this way and have to take medicine for the rest of my life. All the stuff about ministry and complete healing is just me hoping for something but not facing and accepting reality. Maybe it is time to just give up those dreams and let them go for good. Maybe God will not heal me. Then I will no longer have to fight this fight and be discouraged all the time because my hopes are crushed. Just accept life the way it is and be as happy as I can be.

October 24, 2019

I saw an underground dungeon. It was utterly dark, and there was a dark tunnel that led to the dungeon. On top of the ground, I saw Jesus slay the enemies who were guarding the dungeon. Then He came through the dungeon where I was and reached out His hand to me. He was illuminated with light, but everything was dark. I hesitated to take His hand because I was unsure of who He was or if I could trust Him, but I didn't want to stay in the dark dungeon.

I took His hand, and He laced His arm through mine, and we walked through the darkness. There was just enough light from Him to see just the next step in front of us.

Behind us was darkness and in the front of us was darkness. I was shaking and scared, but He was confident and sure. He held a tight grip on me, never loosening it, and comforted me along the way.

As we got closer to the tunnel's opening, light shone into the tunnel. I was closer to freedom. By this time, I felt safer with Him and more confident I could trust Him. Behind us was still pitch black. As I stepped out into full daylight, complete freedom, I threw my arms up, took a deep breath, breathing in the fresh air and hearing the birds sing around me. I twirled around and then hugged Jesus. I looked around and saw all my enemies lying on the ground.

I think this is a clear picture of my journey through this. That starting out, I am not sure who God is, not sure I can trust Him, but as we walk, I begin to know He loves me and that He knows the best path for me. I begin to trust Him more and more with each step. As I come out of this to complete freedom, I will have learned to know His voice. To know His care. To trust He will lead me safely where I need to go. And that Jesus fights for me, and He is ok, even when I am scared and shaky, and He doesn't walk away or leave me just because I am not sure yet. He keeps walking with me and helps me gain more confidence in His love and care for me.

October 2019

I believe that at this moment, God is holding me tighter than He ever has. That He will not let me fall or die in this, but HE is protecting me completely. His arms are wrapped around me like a shield of protection right now. He knows I am vulnerable in my heart right now and that the wounds are raw and need extra protection.

I think about when my boys were small, and they would get sick, and how I wouldn't go far from them during those times.

I always attuned my ears to their voices. I would sleep in the same room with them, and they would get extra attention during those times. I would protect them from others who might bring in other viruses while their immune systems were down and vulnerable. I would give them special food because they wouldn't have much of an appetite. I would do all of this until they were strong again. They rarely got their strength back or their appetite back in one day. It would take time to get them back up and going again.

Psalm 91:4; 15-16 TPT

Verse 4: His massive arms are wrapped around you, protecting you. You can run under his covering of majesty and hide.
His arms of faithfulness are a shield keeping you from harm.

Verses 15-16: I will answer your cry for help every time you pray, and you will find and feel my presence even in your time of pressure and trouble. I will be your glorious hero and give you a feast. You will be satisfied with a full life and with all that I do for you. For you will enjoy the fullness of my salvation!

November 2019

I feel like something beautiful is unfolding in my relationship with God. Something I could never have imagined. I am learning Who He is. I can actually feel myself believing and letting go of my grip. Opening my hand. Realizing that I matter. Maybe I am worth it. That He has been orchestrating a beautiful story all along.

November 6, 2019

I woke up this morning thinking about my journey and trust and the struggle I have with trusting God. It came to my mind about someone who wants to build up their strength. They can't just say a prayer, and God will make their muscles stronger. They have to actually work their muscles. They celebrate little victories along the way as they get stronger. I think it is the same way with trust.

God hasn't just taken this struggle away because it wouldn't make me trust Him anymore if He did. I wouldn't come to know Him and understand who He is, and that He is trustworthy. But walking with me through it and letting me experience who He is and His faithfulness, His love, and grace. Experience His care on every step that works those muscles; it builds that trust. I think about the vision He gave me of Jesus rescuing me from the dungeon.

When Jesus first came and extended His hand to me, I was hesitant to take it. I wasn't sure I could trust Him or who He was. I wasn't sure He had my best interest at heart. I was shaky and afraid, but as we walked along through the dark tunnel, I was more steady because I believed He had good intentions for me, that He did not want to cause me harm, that He would protect me, and that I could trust Him with my life. By the time we reached freedom, I was walking steadily and confidently. I was sure of who He was and that I could trust Him with my life. I was sure His intentions were to help me and not harm me. I believe that is why He isn't doing an immediate miracle in this situation. He is doing so much along the way to build my trust in Him and intimacy with Him. To let my confidence in Him and who He has made me be. He is teaching me to rest and take care of myself because I matter, and I am valuable to Him.

If He were to just take this away in a moment, I would forfeit that beautiful journey of getting to know Him. I would forfeit the dance with Him.

November 6, 2019

"It's not over, don't count yourself out. I am not done with you yet. I am creating a beautiful tapestry, and all will see, and all will know that I am God. I created the Heavens and the earth. I created everything out of nothing, and I am creating beauty from the ashes in your life. Don't rush the story. A beautiful piece of art takes time. It is delicate. It takes precision and delicate brush strokes, but in the end, it is worth the wait, and the artist is proud of their masterpiece. You, My dear daughter, are My masterpiece, and I am at work creating beauty where there has been darkness and pain—faith and trust where there has been fear and doubt. I will make you new inside and out—a story of My love and power for generations to tell.

"I love you so much. You are My baby girl, and you can believe that you hear My voice. The enemy would not speak these things or even want you to hear these things, and you are not making it up. I speak to My children, and you are My child. My voice is kind and compassionate and loving. Don't let the enemy steal these words by making you doubt.

You can trust My words. I will not lead you wrong or promise and not act on your behalf; My words will not return to Me void. I will fulfill all I have said. It may not look the way you think it should, but it will be perfect and always for your best.

You will not regret one moment of the journey when you see the results. Greater than you have dreamed or imagined in your wildest dreams.

"Hold on to Me, sweet girl. I will get you to the other side of this, I promise. It will be worth the pain and the wait. Just hold on. I love you, Your Father."

November 21, 2019

I am starting to feel myself settling into trusting God with this. I believe that He has told me He is going to bring me to the other side of this, and I don't see how or when, or what it will look like, but I know that if He makes a promise, He will fulfill that promise.

Luke 1:45 says, "Blessed is she who believed that the Lord would do what He promised."

God brought to my mind Mark 4:35 when Jesus told the disciples, "Let's go to the other side of the lake."

There was a storm between there and the other side, but even before they got to the other side, Jesus calmed the storm, and 5:1 says, "They came to the other side..."

Psalm 18:30 says, "God's ways are perfect, and all His promises prove true. He is a shield of protection around those who trust Him."

I just know that I am feeling calm and believing He will get me there, despite what I still see in front of me.

November 22. 2019

I was thinking back again to Mark 4:35 and how Jesus was teaching the disciples to trust in the middle before they got to the other side. I know I have said to God before I know I will trust you once you heal me, but I think He is teaching me in the middle to trust before I ever get to the other side. It is in the in-between that I learn He is faithful. I saw myself standing on the other side of the lake, looking back across the lake with tears flowing down my face and seeing the beauty that was in the middle of the storm.

The beauty that was in the journey. Just standing there in awe of Him, in worship of Him because it was in the journey that I really got to know Him and His character. In the journey that so much changed in me. It was in the middle that He held me so tight and comforted me, and proved that He is faithful. Walking away from the edge of that lake with so much gratitude, a completely different person than I was when I started out on the other side. Head held high, shame and guilt washed away, beaming about what God has done.

I was ready to walk into the future hand in hand with my Father and know Him in a way I never would have without the storm.

December 11, 2019

Today I feel like that is where I am. I feel like God is saying to me to take the risk of faith and dare to embrace what He is telling me to do. To strip away all the stuff I have been told I have to do to get healing. To strip away all the old belief systems about who I have been told He is and how He acts. To push through the crowd of voices. The One voice that matters and take a risk on that voice. To let go and shut the door on all the old thinking and beliefs and embrace the new things He is teaching me. To do this His way, rest, trust, enjoy life. Allow Him to love me and heal me in His way, even though it may look contrary to anything I have been taught or told. Shut the door on the old life and step into the new life with Him. Take the risk; it will be worth it. Because for me, it feels like a risk. It feels like a risk to let go of everything I have been taught and embrace something new. Embrace the new picture of God as a loving, kind, compassionate Father, Who wants good for me and has good plans for me. Take the risk. Jesus is waiting, and He has already done everything that needs to be done.

December 18, 2019

It makes me angry when people put God in a box and say He is limited. God is limitless. He has all power and all resources at His fingertips. He can orchestrate anything He wants to orchestrate, anytime, anywhere, for anyone. There are no boundaries or limits to God; He is the God of all creation. He created everything out of nothing! He can change molecular structure, cause limbs to grow, cause the blind to see, the lame to walk, the mute to speak. He can raise the dead. He shuts the mouths of lions and opens up the seas! He is God!! He is the God of the impossible! Do not tell me that there is something that God will not or cannot do!! And don't tell me I have to earn it. Jesus already paid the price when He took the stripes on His back and shed His blood on the cross. Believe BIG! Pray BIG! He loves to give His children good gifts beyond our wildest dreams. Don't let your finite mind limit an infinite God!

6

God Pours Out

Above all, taking the shield of faith with which you will be able to quench all the fiery darts of the wicked one.
- EPHESIANS 6: 16 (NKJV)

Now it is 2020, and as we all know, COVID has hit our nation, and things look so much different than they have ever looked in my lifetime. What would later become a pandemic threw me into a spiral of fear and anxiety once again.

I became one of those people who, because of germs, washed down every item that came from outside my house, didn't allow any visitors, and made everyone sanitize and wash their hands constantly. In fact, I washed my hands so much that they remained cracked and painful much of the time. When wearing a mask became mandatory, I wore one and made anyone entering my house wear one. I was still not going into public places and my husband works from home, so being in lockdown didn't really look much different for us. I kept telling myself, "I'm supposed to have faith and not fear," and, "I'm supposed to believe God is protecting me…" I also said inside, "I'm supposed to believe that if I got COVID-19, God would heal me!" But no matter how often I admonished myself for my fear and apparent lack of faith, I could not stop worrying that me or someone I loved would catch the virus. But I also know God was not mad at me for it. He was not unpleased. God loved me as much as He did anyone else. He understood where I was at and that I was fearful. He could handle it.

A Few Faithful Friends

My son had gotten engaged in February 2020, right before everything shut down. His wedding was set to be in October. I was pretty far along with counseling, to the point that I felt comfortable stopping, though I was still dealing with the anxiety of the virus, which I knew I was not alone in. This was a hard decision because I had become comfortable with my counselor and became used to having our now bi-weekly sessions. I was a little afraid of going backward, but when God moved me out of counseling, He brought a friend back into my life in a greater way. She and I began chatting quite a lot, and she became my confidant. This made the transition from counseling much easier.

Throughout this journey, God has been so faithful to bring

certain individuals alongside me at the exact right time. Sometimes it was a family member. I had one friend who texted me every single day and asked how I was doing. There were many days that I wouldn't have been able to take my medicine or get out of bed without her.

Most of all, my husband and my two boys were my rocks. It was hard at first because my husband didn't understand and had no clue how to deal with what was happening, but there was a point when he came to me and apologized for how he treated me at the beginning of this battle. He has always supported me and been by my side. He was my voice when I couldn't speak. He was my hero when others hurt me. God knew I would need him when he brought him into my life twenty-five years ago.

My two boys were so kind and compassionate even though they were too young to really know or understand what was going on when this started. They loved me through it all. They stood up for me. They had talks with me and made me smile like no one else could. Their hugs made my day. Just seeing their faces gave me a reason to go on. I continued fighting this fight for them.

So here we are, a few months out from my oldest son's wedding. Even with the counseling, I was still not sure if I would make it there. I knew if I didn't, it would send me in a spiral of guilt and shame again. I felt like my family would be disappointed in me once more. My son had expressed his hope that I would make it to the wedding, and I began praying daily that I would.

An Upcoming Ministry

Around August, God began pouring into me promises in a tremendous way, that at this point, I didn't realize I would need to stand on in about a month. He began to speak to me in ways that He had not before. I began having dreams about being in ministry and even writing a book. He began to speak promises to me about my healing and my freedom. He spoke to me about how the severe sickness started in October of 2013, and how October 2020 would be 7 years, and how the number 7 in the Bible represents completion, perfection, and rest. How this would be the year of completion for me. My son's wedding would be in October, beginning the 7th year since the severe sickness began. The following is the journal entry I wrote for this day:

"I had this dream, and I was back in school, and I was trying to fit into all the groups that people try to fit into in school and there kept being this little girl, a little blonde headed girl that sat beside me. She sat beside me a couple times doing different things. The last time she sat beside me, she pulled out this Bible and started reading from it. It was just kind of fragmented stuff that I got, but she started reading and said either cut down or tear down the vine of rejection. Then she said something about debts being canceled, and she said something about Jacob, and then she said something about 55 gods. I was like, okay, this is weird. I don't know what it's supposed to be, but the things I felt like were coming out of that were 1. Cut down the vine of rejection, 2. debt being canceled, 3. Jacob, 4. The number 55, which I feel like God was saying go to Isaiah 55:5."

I felt like that was the 55, and I already had it highlighted on my YouVersion™ Bible. *"You also will command nations you do not know, and people's unknown to you will come running to obey because I the Lord your God the Holy One of Israel have made you glorious."*

I went up in those scriptures a little further just because I was wondering what was before it, and starting at verse 3, it says, *"Come to me with your eyes wide open listen and you will find life, I will make an Everlasting Covenant."* (I just talked about covenant yesterday with someone.) I will give you all the unfailing love I promised to David, See how I used him to display my power among the peoples I made him a leader among the Nations," then 5 says *"you will also command Nations you do not know and people's unknown to you will come running to obey because I the Lord your God, the Holy One of Israel have made you Glorious."*

A couple of things in that; the first part goes back to the root of rejection. The end of that scripture says, *"I the Lord your God, have made you glorious."* I think that is speaking of throughout my life, my big thing has been trying to fit in, trying to be someone I am not, trying to wear the right clothes and have the right house and drive the right car, say the right things and be all these things to please everyone. Rejection was rampant throughout my life, and I never felt like who I was, the Gina that God made me to be, was good enough." I felt I needed to be this classy, suave, sophisticated, rich person that was more than I was, so that last sentence, *"I the Lord your God, the Holy One of Israel have made you glorious,"* fit together for me.

As we go on and I think about the debt cancellation and Jacob, where does that fit in? This is where it gets weird. I looked up debt cancellation in the Bible in Deuteronomy 15. It talks about how they must cancel debt every seven years as well as free the slaves every seven years. God told them to let their land rest, because resting the land caused it to produce better and more abundant crops. While the land rested, it replenished the nutrients in the soil. It was a *sabbath*. God told them that if they followed His commands on this, He would bless them with all He promised, giving them the Land He had promised as their inheritance.

When the slaves were released, they were to be sent out with plenty, not empty-handed. He tells them they will rule over many nations but be ruled by none, which also connects to Isaiah 55:5, which speaks of commanding nations and unknown people running to obey. So, it was all around the number 7.

In the 7th year, the debts were canceled, slaves were set free, and the land rested. I looked up what 7 represents in the Bible, and it said it represents completion, perfection, and rest.

Then we go to Jacob. Jacob had to work for Rachel for 7 years and was given Leah. He then worked another 7 years (for Laban) and was given Rachel. 7 years Jacob worked, 7 years debts canceled, and slaves set free. *7 completion, perfection, and rest.*

I went back to figure out how many years I have been really dealing with the severe anxiety, and I was thinking 2014, but then realized we had to quit the church in October 2013. This year in October will be 7 years, in October is Michael's wedding! *October 2020, 7 years of severe anxiety!*

I told Jason about it, he left the room, and a few minutes later, he returned and showed me the time hop app on his phone. He showed me a post he had posted on Facebook that said, "Sometimes God puts us in a position where our only comfort comes not from what others think, about us, but from what God thinks about us in Christ-that we are forever qualified, delivered, loved, accepted, forgiven, cleansed and approved."

That was a quote from a book he had read, but the amazing

thing was that he posted it 7 years ago! And if that wasn't enough, he posted it at 5:55pm... 7 years, Isaiah 55:5!!! Year of completion, perfection, and rest! October 2020, Michael's wedding, 7 years since I got sick!! I am freaking out!

I thought maybe I could be making it up and connecting things that didn't connect, but then he showed me his phone, and that was the icing on the cake, because that was outside of what I was even connecting. I went to bed last night asking God to speak to me in my dream and give me assurance that He was promising me healing and freedom."

I have never had God speak to me in this way before, making sure that I knew it was Him, and this was the beginning for me of the windows of heaven opening up, and God pouring out profound promises over the next few weeks and months. I didn't know it then, but I was about to need these promises to hold on to and keep me from sinking back to the bottom of the pit. I believe that is why God made it so very obvious to me that it was *Him* speaking. He knew me well enough to know that it would take a lot of assurance for what was coming ahead. I will share some more of these promises with you and explain why I needed them.

7

From My Heart
to the Page

His word was in my heart like a burning fire
Shut up in my bones;
I was weary of holding it back,
And I could not.

- JEREMIAH 20: 9B (NKJV)

The following are actual journal entries that I asked my editor to leave as close to natural as possible so you might hear my heart in "real-time" as I cried out to the Lord in my cycle of struggle and success.

August 22, 2020

So, my son asked what the number 5 meant in the Bible, and his fiancé looked it up, and it meant grace, kindness, and favor, and I have been telling Jason about how I know Jesus has already finished this work by the cross and how He will fulfill His promises to me. I cannot make them happen. Then this morning, I was thinking about the wedding and said to myself, I will get there not by might, nor by power, but by His Spirit. And I started looking into a couple of scriptures I had heard on grace. John 1:16-17 says,

"For from his fullness we have all received, grace upon grace. For the law was given through Moses; grace and truth came through Jesus Christ." John 1:16-17 ESV"

Then the one that really spoke was Zechariah 4:6-10

Then he said to me, "This is the word of the Lord to Zerubbabel: Not by might, nor by power, but by my Spirit, says the Lord of hosts. Who are you, O great mountain? Before Zerubbabel, you shall become a plain. And he shall bring forward the top stone amid shouts of 'Grace, grace to it!'" Then the word of the Lord came to me, saying, "The hands of Zerubbabel have laid the foundation of this house; his hands shall also complete it.

Then you will know that the Lord of hosts has sent me to you. For whoever has despised the day of small things shall rejoice, and shall see the plumb line in the hand of Zerubbabel." Zechariah 4:6-10 ESV

I remembered I had read some commentary on this scripture before, and Zerubbabel is a type of Christ. So I doubled checked that, and sure enough. So I read it using Jesus in the scripture instead of Zerubbabel, and it just reiterated that this is all about Him. He will do this, and His finished work has already paid for it. I love it in the TM,

"The Messenger-Angel said, "Can't you tell?" "No, sir," I said. Then he said, "This is GOD's Message to Zerubbabel: 'You can't force these things. They only come about through my Spirit,' says GOD -of-the-Angel-Armies. 'So, big mountain, who do you think you are? Next to Zerubbabel you're nothing but a molehill. He'll proceed to set the Cornerstone in place, accompanied by cheers: Yes! Yes! Do it!'"

After that, the Word of GOD came to me: "Zerubbabel started rebuilding this Temple and he will complete it. That will be your confirmation that GOD -of-the-Angel-Armies sent me to you. Does anyone dare despise this day of small beginnings? They'll change their tune when they see Zerubbabel setting the last stone in place!" Zechariah 4:6-10."

August 23, 2020

My friend reminded me of when Satan asked Eve, "Did God really say?" and it was like a switch flipped when she said that even though I had heard that before. It was like I was hearing it for the first time.

It made me think about the times I asked God, "What keeps me from believing You are talking to me?" It was like someone pulled back the curtain and exposed the enemy. That is what I hear every time; "Was that really

God? Did I make that up? Did God really say...?"

I saw a picture of like a puppet stage or something, and it had a curtain around it, and then when the curtain was pulled back, it revealed the enemy, and he just looked at me like... *oh no, I have been exposed.*

And I thought I bet Eve felt the same emotion I did... *fear.* Fear that God might not know what is best for her. Fear that God might not be trustworthy. Fear that God might withhold something from her.

I thought there was a movie that had this kind of scene where the curtain had been pulled back. I thought of *The Wizard of Oz* but couldn't place the scene, so I told Jason about it. He said the line from *The Wizard of Oz*, and I knew that was it, so I looked it up. It is a perfect depiction of what was in my head!

When Dorothy and her friends talk to Oz and Toto pulls back the curtain, Oz says, "Pay no attention to the man behind the curtain," and it ends up being a little man!

August 24, 2020

A friend sent me her testimony, and it talked about how God sees the end from the beginning, and I felt like yesterday he was telling me he has been in control of every detail of this battle and every moment of the timing. He proved that when He had my husband post that post 7 years ago at 5:55, knowing I would read it on Friday! In her testimony, she talked about 2 Chronicles 20 and the story of Jehoshaphat and how they praised and defeated their enemies. I just read through 2 Chronicles 20 again. It has been a scripture that God has brought to me several times during this battle. I love that they didn't even have to fight the enemy, but the enemy annihilated themselves! As I sat writing in my journal about all of this this morning, God spoke to me.

I heard Him say, "Gina, it is time to push. You have rested, and now you have come to the end of the pregnancy, and it is time to push. It is time to birth your miracle and step into your destiny, into your calling.

Rise out of the ashes of defeat, fear, and despair. Take your place as a Daughter of the King. It is time to push out this baby. It is time to see the promise fulfilled. Don't be afraid to expect. When a mother is about to see her baby, she gets excited. Don't be afraid to be excited. Don't be afraid to celebrate even before you see the baby. Before you see the promise fulfilled."

I feel like pushing looks like praising through. Praising Him for the promise. Expressing His goodness and power through praise. Praising Him when the enemy is rattling off lies. I believe praise is the gateway to my promise.

The pushing process also requires you to rest between pushing. The rest does not stop. It becomes part of your lifestyle.

Think about what is on the other side of the pushing phase in birth. Knowing that you are about to hold your baby in your arms and see its face gets you through that process. It gives you the strength and determination to keep pushing and not give up. It is the same with this. Thinking about the promise-the freedom and healing that is on the other side of the pushing will give you the strength and determination to not give up. Even on the bad days, just remember what is coming and expect it, and that will produce praise. Thank Him for it now, before it manifests.

See it in your mind as already done. Think of all the things you will do, the food you will eat, the places you will go, the people you will meet, and allow the excitement to come. Allow yourself to feel it!

When a mother expects a baby, she prepares for it. She gets the nursery ready and buys a car seat, and clothes, etc. Prepare for your miracle in your heart and mind, and spirit. Feel the emotions and allow yourself to go there as if it is already done. Because in the spiritual realm, it is already done! Birthing it is just bringing it into the natural realm where you can feel, see, hear, and touch it. You are pushing something from the spiritual realm (inside) to the natural realm (outside). Like a mother pushes a child to the outside where she can see, feel, hear, and touch it.

I felt God saying in my spirit, "Your expectation, which produces praise, will be the catalyst to make that happen. Get excited now. Allow yourself to feel it. Allow yourself to go there. You will not be disappointed! I promise! And I am not a man that I should lie. Why would I take the time to speak to you and spend time with you if it was all a puff of smoke that I did not intend to fulfill? I am not that harsh. I am kind and gentle, and I love to lavish my children with gifts and you, baby girl, are My child, and I love you and want to give you good things.

"Just receive it. Just allow Me to freely and graciously give you freedom and healing. I want to because I love you so much. I love you so much I sent My Son to die for you. Why would I ever withhold anything from you that was for your good? I love you. Please believe Me. Please let yourself believe you hear My voice. It will amaze you how quickly things will change for you when you allow yourself to step into the realm to honestly believe you are hearing from Me. Your life and attitude will be so different. You will never be the same once you allow yourself to believe it is My voice.

"Why would your enemy ever say anything like this to you, and why would you just sit and make this up on your own? Why can't you believe I want to have a conversation with you, just like Jason talks to you? That is a relationship, and that is what I want with you. I want a relationship. To be close to you. That's where you learn to trust, but first, trust that I am speaking and you are hearing. I love you, and I am so excited about what is ahead for you. I am placing people strategically around you who will guard you and be excited with you. Be careful who you share with and who you allow in your bubble because so many will be skeptical, and they will steal away the very excitement that will pull you through.

"Not everyone can handle or comprehend what I am saying to you. This will also be important when you begin a ministry. You will need to choose carefully who you allow in your circle. Not all will be there for the right reasons, and not all will believe or understand, and that is okay; just put a guard around them.

I will give you discernment on this. You will know. I will not leave you to figure it all out on your own. For now, though, just focus on today. Focus on me and what I am saying to you. Focus on the promise you are about to birth. The promise you have been waiting on and carrying inside you for so long. Get ready, it is time to push, baby girl, and I will be right here beside you the whole way."

August 25, 2020

In my head, I was so focused on the wedding that I wasn't really allowing what God is saying and doing to sink in beyond the wedding. Like in my head, all of this was just to get me to the wedding, and then I will wake up the next day and still be where I am now. But this morning it hit me that He is talking about so much more than the wedding. He is saying He is setting me completely free and healing this whole thing beyond that day. He is bringing the entire battle to an end.

I read this scripture in my devotion today, and it stood out to me. Isaiah 51:11 TPT

"Do it again! Those Yahweh has set free will return to Zion and come celebrating with songs of joy! They will be crowned with never-ending joy! Gladness and joy will overwhelm them; despair and depression will disappear!"

Then I read from 11-16 in my NLT

"Those who have been ransomed by the Lord will

return. They will enter Jerusalem singing, crowned with everlasting joy. Sorrow and mourning will disappear, and they will be filled with joy and gladness. "I, yes I, am the one who comforts you. So why are you afraid of mere humans, who wither like the grass and disappear? Yet you have forgotten the Lord, your Creator, the one who stretched out the sky like a canopy and laid the foundations of the earth. Will you remain in constant dread of human oppressors? Will you continue to fear the anger of your enemies? Where is their fury and anger now? It is gone! Soon all you captives will be released! Imprisonment, starvation, and death will not be your fate! For I am the Lord your God, who stirs up the sea, causing its waves to roar. My name is the Lord of Heaven's Armies. And I have put my words in your mouth and hidden you safely in my hand. I stretched out the sky like a canopy and laid the foundations of the earth. I am the one who says to Israel, 'You are my people!'"

I like vs. 14 also in TPT:

"Those who are suffering will soon be released. They will not die in their dark dungeon, nor will they go hungry."

Which was interesting to me. It talks about 2 of my fears, dying in the middle of this, and the food!

I was putting together a puzzle and was listening to a song called *Miracle Maker.* Suddenly, the Holy Spirit just hit me really strongly, so I got up and went to my room and got on my knees and started worshipping and laughing and crying and then played a song that I had put in a folder by itself just the day before called Healing Oil.

It says, "I can feel His healing oil running down my brow. I wouldn't trade another lifetime for how I feel right now."

Suddenly God's presence got so strong in the room. He was right there with me, and I saw a vision of Jesus laying his hands on my head, and I just broke. My face went down to the ground because His presence was so strong. I felt Him say, "I am healing you, and this is just the beginning."

I wasn't thinking about anything at this moment, it was like time just stood still and I was crying from a deep, deep place. He was doing deep, deep work, and it came in waves. This was definitely a powerful encounter with Jesus!

August 26, 2020

God took me to the book of Joshua this morning. First, He spoke to me about them crossing the Jordan River and how God told them the Ark of the Covenant, which represented God's presence and Spirit, would lead them. How His presence and Spirit will lead me across my Jordan. Then He started talking to me about labels. How life and people have put specific labels on me, I have lived my life out of.

Some of these labels were broken, sick, poor, less than, plain, forgettable, guilty, shameful, fearful, shy, timid, afraid, replaceable weak. But He is pulling those labels off and putting what He says about me on my life, and I will begin to live out of those labels.

The labels He puts on me are, free, healed, chosen, called, a mighty Daughter of the King, beautiful, strong, more than enough, brave, courageous, wise, unforgettable, irreplaceable, exquisite, approved, valuable, worthy, righteous, forgiven, clean, unashamed, accepted, pleasing, priceless.

God spoke to me about how He chose and called Joshua to lead the people of Israel and how He told him not to be afraid or discouraged because He would be with him, and where he set his foot, He would give him that ground. God told Him He would not fail him or abandon him.

He told him to be strong and courageous and lead the people to possess their promised land. God said that it is time for me, like Joshua, to rise up and become who he made me to be before I was even born, to lead and not follow. That I have what it takes that He uses the small things and the things the world sees as foolish to confound the wise.

I am not who I thought I was. I am not who the world and life have labeled me to be. There is so much more on the inside that is ready to be birthed to the outside. God is birthing more than just healing and freedom, but also the manifestation of my new identity. The one He says I am. I will lead people to their promise land. He told Joshua to have the priest carry the Ark out into the river, and when their feet touched the water, the flow of water would be cut off upstream, and the river would stand like a wall, so the people could cross. That is what He is calling me to. To step into the water first so that others can cross on dry ground. To be a leader forging the way for the broken and forgotten.

He said that He will be with me. I will walk in a new confidence. Knowing my new identity in Him. Knowing my Father loves me, taking care of me, and giving that same confidence to others. Knowing that I am a Daughter of the Most High God, The Commander of Angel Armies. It is time to rise up and take my position as His daughter.

I, like Esther, have been chosen for such a time as this to lead people to freedom. To forge the way across the river and see lives saved. They will no longer drown. It is time for me to believe that I am worth more than I thought I was, and I am stronger and braver than I think I am, and my voice, wisdom, and opinion matter. It doesn't matter how I feel or what anyone says; the only thing that matters is that He is calling me. He has chosen me.

God chooses whom He will choose and doesn't care about man's opinion on it. He is God. He spoke through a donkey; he can definitely speak through this little country girl. Don't count myself out. Rise up and take my place in the kingdom. And just like He promised Joshua, He will be with me wherever I go. He will lead and guide me, watch over my footsteps, and give me the land I place my feet on. I will take land for His kingdom from the grips of the enemy.

The enemy is scared of me because he knows better than I who I am and the power and authority God has given me, and He knows my Daddy.

Stand up! Rise up! Square your shoulders, hold your head high. Take your place and let your voice be heard.

I have to get the picture of me as weak and small out of my mind. I have see myself as strong in the Lord and the power of His might. See me as called and chosen, standing tall. One trembling heart and soul becomes a servant bold and courageous!

In my prayer time today, God spoke again. I forgot that when I woke up, I had Isaiah on my mind as well. It is a weird story because when this thing started on Friday, I noticed we needed some new tongs, and I ordered some on Amazon, which was supposed to be here today. So when God brought Isaiah to my mind, the scripture talked about the angel touching Isaiah's lips with tongs. Then one of the seraphim flew to me with a burning coal he had taken from the altar with a pair of tongs. He touched my lips with it and said, "See, this coal has touched your lips. Now your guilt is removed, and your sins are forgiven."

Then I heard the Lord asking, "Whom should I send as a messenger to this people? Who will go for us?"

I said, "Here I am. Send me."

So I told God I was overwhelmed and didn't know why He would choose me, but that I would say yes to His call. Then I heard, "You will prophesy to nations," and when I heard that, I was like, um, God is this you? Because that is scary.

And He said, "It will not be you, it will be Me working through you."

Immediately my mind went to Jeremiah 1:5-12:

"I knew you before I formed you in your mother's womb. Before you were born, I set you apart and appointed you as my prophet to the nations."

"O Sovereign Lord," I said, "I can't speak for You! I'm too young!"

The Lord replied, "Don't say, 'I'm too young,' for you must go wherever I send you and say whatever I tell you. And don't be afraid of the people, for I will be with you and will protect you. I, the Lord, have spoken!"

Then the Lord reached out and touched my mouth and said, "Look, I have put my words in your mouth! Today I appoint you to stand up against nations and kingdoms. Some you must uproot and tear down, destroy and overthrow. Others you must build up and plant." Then the Lord said to me, "Look, Jeremiah! What do you see?"

And I replied, "I see a branch from an almond tree."

And the Lord said, "That's right, and it means that I am watching, and I will certainly carry out all my plans."

Then I remembered the verses He gave me yesterday in Isaiah 51:12 & 16:

"I, yes I, am the one who comforts you. So why are you afraid of mere humans, who wither like the grass and disappear?" And, "I have put my words in your mouth and hidden you safely in My hand, I stretched out the sky like a canopy and laid the foundations of the earth. I am the one who says to Israel, 'You are My people!'"

I am just like, am I really hearing this? Am I in my body right now, or is this even real life? Instead of saying I am too young, I would say I am too old, too shy, or too afraid.

I am so scared of messing this up, but I keep hearing God say, you can't mess this up because I am doing this, not you. And when I want to figure it out, He just says, "Let me unfold it, and when you need to move, I will tell you."

Yesterday in my prayer time, God gave me Isaiah 61, and it was like a progression of Jesus heals me and sets me free, and then He sends me out.

"The Spirit of the Sovereign Lord is upon me, for the Lord has anointed me to bring good news to the poor. He has sent me to comfort the brokenhearted and to proclaim that captives will be released and prisoners will be freed. He has sent me to tell those who mourn that the time of the Lord's favor has come, and with it, the day of God's anger against their enemies. To all who mourn in Israel, he will give a crown of beauty for ashes, a joyous blessing instead of mourning, festive praise instead of despair. In their righteousness, they will be like great oaks that the Lord has planted for his own glory. They will rebuild the ancient ruins, repairing cities destroyed long ago.

"They will revive them, though they have been deserted for many generations. Foreigners will be your servants. They will feed your flock and plow your fields and tend your vineyards. You will be called priests of the Lord, ministers of our God.

"You will feed on the treasures of the nations and boast in their riches. Instead of shame and dishonor, you will enjoy a double share of honor. You will possess a double portion of prosperity in your land, and everlasting joy will be yours. "For I, the Lord, love justice. I hate robbery and wrongdoing. I will faithfully reward my people for their suffering and make an everlasting covenant with them. Their descendants will be recognized and honored among the nations.

"Everyone will realize that they are a people the Lord has blessed."

"I am overwhelmed with joy in the Lord my God! For he has dressed me with the clothing of salvation and draped me in a robe of righteousness.

I am like a bridegroom dressed for his wedding or a bride with her jewels. The Sovereign Lord will show his justice to the nations of the world. Everyone will praise him! His righteousness will be like a garden in early spring, with plants springing up everywhere."

Then this morning, I woke up, and He told me to read about Paul and Silas in prison. He has been talking to me about praise and having expectancy and anticipation and excitement.

Acts 16:23-26: "They were severely beaten, and then they were thrown into prison. The jailer was ordered to make sure they didn't escape. So the jailer put them into the inner dungeon and clamped their feet in the stocks. Around midnight Paul and Silas were praying and singing hymns to God, and the other prisoners were listening. Suddenly, there was a massive earthquake, and the prison was shaken to its foundations. All the doors immediately flew open, and the chains of every prisoner fell off!"

Then it says that the jailer and his whole family were saved.

I felt like God was saying, there are so many people listening and watching me on this journey, and as I praise Him and live with excitement and expectancy, not only are my chains going to fall off but the chains of many around me. It will have a ripple effect through people I know and people I will minister to.

I also saw a vision of a dam or a wall, and it had a crack in it, and there was water building up behind it. As the water pressure kept pushing against it, it got weaker and weaker and lost its strength, and suddenly the whole thing broke open, and the water just rushed through.

I feel like God is saying that the wall the enemy has built has a crack in it and is getting weaker and weaker.

God is just pouring in and pouring in His Spirit, and suddenly because of the build-up and pressure against it, it will just burst open, and things will happen quickly.

In those scriptures in Acts 16, it talked about SUDDENLY there was an earthquake, and the chains fell off.

I woke up yesterday morning with Jeremiah 29:11 from the TM on my mind and heard God say to read Isaiah 30:25.

"This is GOD's Word on the subject: I know what I'm doing. I have it all planned out—plans to take care of you, not abandon you, plans to give you the future you hope for." Jeremiah 29:11 TM

"In that day, when your enemies are slaughtered, and the towers fall, there will be streams of water flowing down every mountain and hill." Isaiah 30:25 NLT"

I was reading about how water in the Bible can represent life and refreshing and healing. Took me back to the picture He gave me of the dam bursting and water gushing through. We were watching Elevation Church, and they sang the song "There is a Cloud." And again, it was about water. The song talked about the dry season is over, and there was a line in there that went:

"And with great anticipation
We await the Promise to come
Everything that You have spoken
Will come to pass, let it be done!"

Then a pastor came up and started talking about how what you see in your circumstances does not match what you see in your spirit. He talked about how Elijah keeps being persistent looking for rain.

He said we should be persistent and keep seeing the promise fulfilled even before we actually see it in the natural. He talked about streams coming into dry places. He was also talking about how our salvation is done, and yet it is *being done*. How God gives us *progressive revelation.*

God spoke to me that is what is happening with my healing. That is why I keep feeling it is already done. It *is* done, but at the same time, it is being worked out. It is that picture of pushing it from the inside out.

He talked about how we can know something, but do we believe it. And how He gives us a new perspective and aspect of who He is in the middle of our problems. Not only does He want to do a miracle, but He wants to show us who He is.

I went back and read that story of Elijah expecting rain and realized he sent the servant 7 times. The 7th time, there was a cloud, and then quickly, the rain came.

It took me back to my 7's from the other day. Jason and I talked about how I am scared to get excited and believe again. I have allowed myself to go there in the past and been disappointed. But I felt like God was saying dare to believe again.

With that story and the 7 being the number of completion and perfection, I felt God was saying, "Believe again, this is the time for completion."

August 31, 2020

    I believe God is showing me there is going to be a moment where my mind and my spirit just finally connect, and this thing will be complete. There is water trickling through the crack in that dam, and before long, the pressure of that water is going to cause it to burst open. And the healing and freedom will just flow through, and then it will also flow into the lives around me, causing streams and rivers and pools to form in dry places of people's lives. These are some of my verses for today.

    "So David went to Baal-perazim and defeated the Philistines there. "The Lord did it!" David exclaimed. "He burst through my enemies like a raging flood!" So he named that place Baal-perazim (which means "the Lord who bursts through")." 2 Samuel 5:20 NLT

    "I will open up rivers for them on the high plateaus. I will give them fountains of water in the valleys. I will fill the desert with pools of water. Rivers fed by springs will flow across the parched ground. I will plant trees in the barren desert— cedar, acacia, myrtle, olive, cypress, fir, and pine. I am doing this, so all who see this miracle will understand what it means— that it is the Lord who has done this, the Holy One of Israel who created it." Isaiah 41:18-20 NLT

God was speaking to me yesterday and last night. He said to me yesterday to step out of the darkness and into the light, and in Isaiah 49:9, it says, "I will say to the prisoners, come out in freedom. And to those in darkness, come into the light." I looked up the commentary on this scripture, and it says some translations say, "reveal or show yourself," and that it indicates stepping into the Sun of Righteousness. Which reminded me of the scripture, "But for you who fear my name, the Sun of Righteousness will rise with healing in his wings. And you will go free, leaping with joy like calves let out to pasture." Malachi 4:2 NLT

And then I also read John 1:5.
"The light shines in the darkness, and the darkness can never extinguish it." John 1:5 NLT

I wasn't sure what God was saying until about 11pm last night, and He began to reveal it to me. He said it is time to step out of the old identity and leave this season behind. It is time to leave behind the past. Leave behind the shame, fear, anxiety, and guilt. It is time to step into the light, into my new identity in Christ. He said I have been lurking in the shadows long enough with my head hung down in guilt, fear, and shame. Shrinking back from who He made me to be. It is time for me to step into my place and shine and walk with my head held high and my shoulders squared, knowing Whose I am and who I am. "It's in Christ that we find out who we are and what we are living for." Ephesians 1:11 TM

This reminded me of Him saying He was pulling off old labels and putting on new ones. It also took me back to the dream where He said to cut down the vine of rejection. So around midnight, He started speaking again. I asked Him why did you say "vine of rejection" instead of root? I usually hear someone say root.

He said because the branches are attached to the vine, and the vine determines what kind of fruit the branch will produce. You were producing fruit from the vine of rejection, which was fear, shame, guilt, anxiety, and getting your identity from that instead of from the vine of Christ. My roots were in God, but my vine was foreign to the tree. It was an intruder.

When you sever the vine of rejection and graft into the vine of Christ, you will begin to produce fruit from that identity, love, joy, peace, etc.

I thought about John 15, where He talks about Him being the vine and us the branches, and we abide in Him. Then also Romans 11:17 NLT, "But some of these branches from Abraham's tree—some of the people of Israel—have been broken off. And you Gentiles, who were branches from a wild olive tree, have been grafted in. So now you also receive the blessing God has promised Abraham and his children, sharing in the rich nourishment from the root of God's special olive tree."

Because my vine was rejection, all my fear and anxiety symptoms were being produced. The enemy had me fighting the physical symptoms and telling me it was because of what I was eating or some severe illness.

That it was all my fault and kept throwing up smokescreens and focusing on the symptoms to keep me from seeing his deception and seeing the truth. That takes me back to the scene of The Wizard of Oz where he is exposed for who he is.

"Rise from the dust, O Jerusalem. Sit in a place of honor. Remove the chains of slavery from your neck, O captive daughter of Zion." Isaiah 52:2 NLT

I know it is done!! I don't know when it will burst through from the spiritual to the natural, but I know it is done.

I will rise up and take my position as a daughter of the King and walk in the calling and identity that He called me to before I was ever born.

"Listen to me, all you in distant lands! Pay attention, you who are far away! The Lord called me before my birth; from within the womb, he called me by name." Isaiah 49:1 NLT

I don't know how it will manifest, but I know I am healed, whole and free. And I will step out of the shadows into the light!

I keep getting these moments where I just start laughing and crying and feel like I will burst. I keep hearing in my spirit; I see it, see the cloud, and it is coming. Just like the story of the rain and Elijah! I believe in their moments of joy and laughter; it is His presence, and the chains are breaking!"

September 2, 2020

Today I heard in my spirit, "I hear it, I hear the voice of triumph!" He took me back to Jericho, and Elijah, and Naaman. All these miracles happened on the 7th time, and 7 is the number of completion and perfection. In my mind, it is hard to comprehend that God can actually, in an instant, change everything or make me able to eat or heal my body, etc.

I have believed so many times, but they had to keep believing for these miracles after the 1st time, the 2nd time, and the 6th time. God is saying to me, allow yourself to believe again. This is the 7th year of severe anxiety. Believe it again!

Also, none of these miracles could have been comprehended in the natural mind, and none of them made any sense. The enemy is fighting hard today to get me to give up, but I saw a picture of myself digging my feet into the dirt and being tenacious like I am not moving devil. I may be little, but so was David, and he defeated his giant, not him, but God! I will be like a bulldog with a bone, and I will not move.

September 4, 2020

The last two days, there has been so much doubt trying to come in. One lady told me I needed to go out and do something to prove and test my faith, or otherwise, how would I know that I was healed? God hasn't told me that. He has told me to stand still and see His deliverance and to just believe.

What works for someone else may not be what God wants to do in my life or what someone thinks I should do. God took me to the lady with the issue of blood. It says that she felt her bleeding stop immediately.

"Immediately the bleeding stopped, and she could feel in her body that she had been healed of her terrible condition." Mark 5:29

God has been using those kinds of words in regards to my healing, "suddenly the water will bursts through the dam." He gave me the scripture where David said, "the Lord bursts through my enemies like a raging flood."

In a moment, something can change. There will be a moment when it all just clicks like a switch was flipped. I will step out of the darkness into the light.

The lady with the issue of blood didn't have to prove she was, healed. She felt it immediately in her body. I have been in my head trying to figure out, if this is really God speaking, because it seems impossible, and it seems like, how can He suddenly set my mind free and heal my body? But I have to get out of my head and into my spirit.

The fall of Jericho, Elijah and the rainstorm, and Naaman dipping in the Jordan River, all miracles that seemed foolish to the people around them, and probably even to themselves, but they believed God would do it. So they obeyed what He said, and they saw their miracle.

Mary, and The Day of Pentecost, and Zerubbabel. Mary asked the angel the same question I have asked: how will this happen? It seems impossible.

The angel answered that the Holy Spirit would come upon her and the power of the Holy Spirit would overshadow her.

"Mary asked the angel, 'But how can this happen? I am a virgin.' The angel replied, 'The Holy Spirit will come upon you, and the power of the Most High will overshadow you. So the baby to be born will be holy, and he will be called the Son of God.'" Luke 1:34-35.

It happened that way without her doing anything except believing He would do what He said. "You are blessed because you believed that the Lord would do what he said." Luke 1:45 The Holy Spirit came upon her, and she conceived Jesus.

On the day of Pentecost, it says there was a sound as of a mighty rushing wind, Acts 2:2, which God brought to my mind the other day when I said, I hear it, I hear the voice of triumph. And the Holy Spirit settled on them in the upper room, and something supernatural happened. They believed it would happen like Jesus told them, and they waited.

"Suddenly, there was a sound from heaven like the roaring of a mighty windstorm, and it filled the house where they were sitting." Acts 2:2

With Zerubbabel, God told him, it would not be by might, nor by power, but by His Spirit and that nothing, not even a mighty mountain in front of him, would stand in his way.

Zechariah 4:6-7, "Then he said to me, 'This is what the Lord says to Zerubbabel: It is not by force nor by strength, but by my Spirit, says the Lord of Heaven's Armies. Nothing, not even a mighty mountain, will stand in Zerubbabel's way; it will become a level plain before him!'"

Then I read about Abraham in The Message Bible (TM) in Romans 4. Here are the things that stood out to me.

"If Abraham, by what he did for God, got God to approve him, he could certainly have taken credit for it. But the story we're given is a God-story, not an Abraham-story. What we read in Scripture is, 'Abraham entered into what God was doing for him, and that was the turning point. He trusted God to set him right instead of trying to be right on his own.'

If you're a hard worker and do a good job, you deserve your pay; we don't call your wages a gift. But if you see that the job is too big for you, that it's something only God can do, and you trust him to do it—you could never do it for yourself no matter how hard and long you worked—well, that trusting-him-to-do-it is what gets you set right with God, by God. Sheer gift.

That famous promise God gave Abraham—that he and his children would possess the earth—was not given because of something Abraham did or would do.

It was based on God's decision to put everything together for him, which Abraham then entered when he believed.

If those who get what God gives them only get it by doing everything they are told to do and filling out all the right forms properly signed, that eliminates personal trust completely and turns the promise into an ironclad contract!

That's not a holy promise; that's a business deal. A contract drawn up by a hard-nosed lawyer and with plenty of fine print only makes sure that you will never be able to collect. But if there is no contract in the first place, simply a promise—and God's promise at that— you can't break it. This is why the fulfillment of God's promise depends entirely on trusting God and his way and then simply embracing him and what he does. God's promise arrives as pure gift.

We call Abraham 'father' not because he got God's attention by living like a saint, but because God made something out of Abraham when he was a nobody. Isn't that what we've always read in Scripture, God saying to Abraham, 'I set you up as father of many peoples.'? Abraham was first named 'father' and then became a father because he dared to trust God to do what only God could do: raise the dead to life, with a word make something out of nothing.

When everything was hopeless, Abraham believed anyway, deciding to live not on the basis of what he saw he couldn't do but on what God said he would do.

And so he was made father of a multitude of peoples. God himself said to him, 'You're going to have a big family, Abraham!'

Abraham didn't focus on his own impotence and say, 'It's hopeless. This hundred-year-old body could never father a child.' Nor did he survey Sarah's decades of infertility and give up. He didn't tiptoe around God's promise asking cautiously skeptical questions. He plunged into the promise and came up strong, ready for God, sure that God would make good on what he had said.

That's why it is said, 'Abraham was declared fit before God by trusting God to set him right.' But it's not just Abraham; it's also us! The same thing gets said about us when we embrace and believe the One who brought Jesus to life when the conditions were equally hopeless. The sacrificed Jesus made us fit for God, set us right with God." (Romans 4, TM)

This tells me that all Abraham did to receive His promise is believe that God would do what He said He would do and what He could only do. God raises the dead to life and calls things into existence that do not exist. He can change cells and atoms in my body and molecular structures in my brain, not because I do something to earn it, but because Jesus paid the price for it at the cross and I believe in Him, and I believe in the ability and power of God to bring it to pass.

He did for the woman with the issue of blood. He did it for Mary, He did it on the day of Pentecost, and He did it for Abraham. It was purely the work of the Holy Spirit falling, and suddenly everything changes.

I feel like God is calling me to simply believe that He is going to do what He has promised He would do and when I plunge into that promise with all I have, my life will never be the same, suddenly, in a moment, everything can be made new and restored. This is what I believe He is asking me to believe for because this is what I believe He is saying He is going to do."

September 5, 2020

Today, God is saying that nothing is impossible for Him, that He is God.

"Who else has held the oceans in his hand? Who has measured off the heavens with his fingers? Who else knows the weight of the earth or has weighed the mountains and hills on a scale? Who is able to advise the Spirit of the Lord? Who knows enough to give him advice or teach him? Has the Lord ever needed anyone's advice? Does he need instruction about what is good? Did someone teach him what is right or show him the path of justice?

"No, for all the nations of the world are but a drop in the bucket.

They are nothing more than dust on the scales. He picks up the whole earth as though it were a grain of sand. To whom will you compare me? Who is my equal?" asks the Holy One. "Look up into the heavens. Who created all the stars? He brings them out like an army, one after another, calling each by its name.

Because of his great power and incomparable strength, not a single one is missing. O Jacob, how can you say the Lord does not see your troubles? O Israel, how can you say God ignores your rights? Have you never heard? Have you never understood? The Lord is the everlasting God, the Creator of all the earth. He never grows weak or weary. No one can measure the depths of his understanding. He gives power to the weak and strength to the powerless. Even youths will become weak and tired, and young men will fall in exhaustion." Isaiah 40:12-15; 25-30.

That His ways are not my ways. "My thoughts are nothing like your thoughts," says the Lord. "And my ways are far beyond anything you could imagine. For just as the heavens are higher than the earth, so my ways are higher than your ways and my thoughts higher than your thoughts." Isaiah 55:8-9

He keeps saying in the scriptures I have been reading that He is coming to defeat my enemies. "A thunderous voice cries out in the wilderness: 'Prepare the way for Yahweh's arrival! Make a highway straight through the desert for our God! Look!

Here comes Lord Yahweh as a victorious warrior; he triumphs with his awesome power. Watch as he brings with him his reward and the spoils of victory to give to his people. He will care for you as a shepherd tends his flock, gathering the weak lambs and taking them in his arms. He carries them close to his heart and gently leads those that have young.'" Isaiah 40:3; 10

This reminds me of what I heard in my spirit the other night; I heard the voice of triumph. It was God's voice!

"Say to those with fearful hearts, 'Be strong, and do not fear, for your God is coming to destroy your enemies. He is coming to save you.'" Isaiah 35:4

"The Spirit of the Sovereign Lord is upon me, for the Lord has anointed me to bring good news to the poor. He has sent me to comfort the brokenhearted and to proclaim that captives will be released and prisoners will be freed. He has sent me to tell those who mourn that the time of the Lord's favor has come, and with it, the day of God's anger against their enemies. To all who mourn in Israel, he will give a crown of beauty for ashes, a joyous blessing instead of mourning, festive praise instead of despair. In their righteousness, they will be like great oaks that the Lord has planted for his own glory." Isaiah 61:1-3

"So David went to Baal-perazim and defeated the Philistines there. "The Lord did it!" David exclaimed. "He burst through my enemies like a raging flood!"

So he named that place Baal-perazim (which means "the Lord who bursts through")." 2 Samuel 5:20

And He is going to set me completely free from the fear of dying because Jesus died for me to be free from it.

"Since, therefore, [these His] children share in flesh and blood [in the physical nature of human beings], He [Himself] in a similar manner partook of the same [nature], that by [going through] death He might bring to nought and make of no effect of him who had the power of death—that is, the devil—And also that He might deliver and completely set free all those who through the [haunting] fear of death were held in bondage throughout the whole course of their lives" Hebrews 2:14-15 AMP

This is not something I can do myself. I cannot set myself free, but I believe He will do it, but He is saying to me to just wait patiently and expectantly for Him. I do know that it is already happening. I told Jason today that I know that Jesus holds the keys to death, and the devil (or no one else) has the power to take me out of this world, only Jesus, and that when He does, I know I will go to heaven. I said that it has to be God giving me that thought because that is not a natural thought for me.

I have been scared to say that because I am always afraid that God will let me die as soon as I am not scared of death.

I know, though, that God has not brought me this far and given me promises about the future He has for me and that He will use me if I was just going to die as soon as He set me free. That would be very cruel and would not bring Him glory at all. He has promised me that He has a future ministry for me, so I do not believe He would just let me die now. But I have to be patient and wait for Him and not try to do this on my own.

"But those who wait for the Lord [who expect, look for, and hope in Him] shall change and renew their strength and power; they shall lift their wings and mount up [close to God] as eagles [mount up to the sun]; they shall run and not be weary, they shall walk and not faint or become tired. I do not believe it is going to be long." Isaiah 40:31 AMP

"For since the world began, no ear has heard, and no eye has seen a God like you, who works for those who wait for him!" Isaiah 64:4.

"I waited patiently for the Lord to help me, and he turned to me and heard my cry. He lifted me out of the pit of despair, out of the mud and the mire. He set my feet on solid ground and steadied me as I walked along. He has given me a new song to sing, a hymn of praise to our God. Many will see what he has done and be amazed. They will put their trust in the Lord." Psalm 40:1-3

"[What, what would have become of me] had I not believed that I would see the Lord's goodness in the land of the living! Wait and hope for and expect the Lord; be brave and of good courage and let your heart be stout and enduring. Yes, wait for and hope for and expect the Lord." Psalm 27:13-14 AMP.

God is saying to me that I cannot earn this. I cannot make it happen or conjure it up or manufacture something. He is doing this, not me. He made the promise, and He will fulfill it. This morning He gave me these scriptures.

"For the Lord is the Spirit, and wherever the Spirit of the Lord is, there is freedom." 2 Corinthians 3:17

"So Christ has truly set us free. Now make sure that you stay free and don't get tied up again in slavery to the law." Galatians 5:1

He said, "If what someone says puts you in bondage and does not set you free, you know it is not My Spirit."

8

Death and Life

But You, O Lord, are a shield for me,
My glory and the One who lifts up my head.
- PSALM 3:3 (NKJV)

Things began to take another turn. On September 7th, 2020, my husband's dad was taken to the hospital at 4am because he was incoherent and had a high fever. This began a dark time for us that would last two weeks. Even before this, my father-in-law suffered liver and stomach problems and had trouble keeping his blood count up, but we thought he was doing okay, all things considered. Unfortunately, that was not the case.

First, they told us he had an infection in his gallbladder that had turned into sepsis. He was not progressing very well initially but then had a turn for the better where he recognized his wife and my husband and they were able to speak to him in brief spurts. They were preparing everything to send him to a rehabilitation facility upon his release from the hospital. His doctor released him from ICU, and then suddenly, he began getting fluid in his abdomen. The medical staff determined he had to stay, and they kept having to drain off the fluid that continued to accumulate.

On September 21st, my husband got the call he did not want to get. The doctor told him that his dad had taken a turn for the worst, and they did not expect him to make it. They were preparing him for end-of-life care, and he and his mom needed to come to the hospital to go over the details and possibly see him for the last time. They didn't know if he had hours or days left. During this time, I could not go to the hospital with him because of the COVID restrictions. So, I stayed home with my boys and waited for the call. Around 2 am the next morning, Jason walked in, and I knew it was not good. His dad had passed away in the night. Jason said that his dad expressed to him a few days before that he "just wanted to die."

This was a moment where God absolutely took over for me. In the natural, I should have fallen apart and spiraled, but only by God's strength and grace was I able to pull myself up and take control for my husband, who now needed me to be his shoulder. After he was my shoulder for so long now, I could not let him down. This was one of my biggest fears; what would I do if one of our parents passed away? Would I be able to handle it? Well, I was about to find out that with God, I could do it.

I wish I could explain to you how I got through the next few days of planning the funeral and talking him and his mom through details, but all I can say to you is God showed up for me right when I needed Him. He was my strength and breath every moment. All of us were running on little to no sleep, and typically my body would not have been able to handle this, but again, somehow, God got me through. This was when all the promises God had been pouring in became my strength and ground to stand on. I knew that God would not promise me all those things and then let me down. He is not a man that He should or can lie. So, I put everything I had (even though some days it wasn't much) into believing that I would make it through this crisis.

Jason with his parents in January 2020.

GOD'S PEACE TRANSCENDS

Was there any anxiety and fear? ABSOLUTELY! But the difference was that this time, it did not take me out. I did not allow it to win. How? All I can say is, *God was there.*

Philippians 4:7 came alive to me, that His peace that transcends all understanding guarded my heart and mind and emotions.

"And God's peace [shall be yours, that tranquil state of a soul assured of its salvation through Christ, and so fearing nothing from God and being content with its earthly lot of whatever sort that is, that peace] which transcends all understanding shall garrison and mount guard over your hearts and minds in Christ Jesus." Philippians 4:7 AMPC

It is so true that God always brings good out of bad. What looked like death, God used to bring life. On September 16th, 2020, I had written this in my journal:

The one who calls to me: Arise, my dearest. Hurry, my darling. Come away with me! I have come as you have asked to draw you to my heart and lead you out. For now is the time, my beautiful one. The season has changed. The bondage of your barren winter has ended, and the season of hiding is over and gone. The rains have soaked the earth and left it bright with blossoming flowers. The season for singing and pruning the vines has arrived. I hear the cooing of doves in our land, filling the air with songs to awaken you and guide you forth.

Can you not discern this new day of destiny breaking forth around you? The early signs of my purposes everywhere. The fragrance of their flowers whispers, 'There is change in the air.' Arise, my love, my beautiful companion, and run with me to the higher place. For now, is the time to arise and come away with me." Song of Songs 2:10-13 TPT.

My season was changing. What looked like death God had brought life out of. While one soul left this earth to be with Jesus, another soul was awakened and began to live again. My father-in-law's death was the moment life began to burst in me again. Although he will be missed, his laughter and his love for Jesus lives on, and he will always be a part of my story.

God spoke this to me the same day He gave me the scripture from Song of Songs: "This is what God says, the God who builds a road right through the ocean, who carves a path through pounding waves. The God who summons horses and chariots and armies—they lie down and then can't get up; they're snuffed out like so many candles: Forget about what's happened; don't keep going over old history. Be alert, be present. I'm about to do something brand-new. It's bursting out! Don't you see it? There it is! I'm making a road through the desert, rivers in the badlands. Wild animals will say 'Thank you!'—the coyotes and the buzzards—Because I provided water in the desert, rivers through the sunbaked earth, drinking water for the people I chose, the people I made especially for myself, a people custom-made to praise me." Isaiah 43:16-21

Then I sat down to write, and this is what I heard God say:

"This is the end of one season. We are closing the door and ending this chapter. The season of this battle is over, and we are stepping into a new season. A season of joy and life like never before. A season of freedom. Harvesting all the tears and sorrows that were planted in this season."

This is not the end, but only the beginning. The enemy formed this weapon, and God has used it to sift through and burn off the things that would hinder me in my next season. I am about to step into a season of prosperity and laughter (Hunter, my son, reminded me that no weapon formed against me will prosper...see Isaiah 54 below), a season of joy instead of mourning. Beauty instead of ashes. Light instead of darkness. A season of coming alongside others and sharing my story to help them find healing in their dry season. It is a season where rain will fall abundantly and bring refreshing and new life, not only for my family and me but to those around me.

"Let the joy come now. Chains are breaking. Can you hear them falling to the ground? One by one, all the enemy's plans are being thwarted. My plans for you are being unveiled and revealed. Stay close to Me as we transition into this new season in your life.

"You will need My direction, My voice to guide you because I am taking you to places you have never been. I will show you things you have never seen, and you will do things you never dreamed you would do, and you and your household and the whole family will be filled with abundant joy and laughter as you look back over what the Lord has done in your life.

"It will be a monument, a cornerstone, for generations to come in your family. How one trembling heart and soul became a servant bold and courageous because she chose to believe in a God Who loves her extravagantly, and chose to believe He cared and loved her enough to do the impossible in her life, so she took the risk of faith and stepped into her destiny. She took her moment and her place in history.

"This is the legacy you will leave as you dare to believe and stay close to me. I AM all you will need!"

I felt like God was saying, "Winter is over, and you are stepping into My purposes and plans for you. It has felt like everything was dead and frozen over. The leaves and the trees were brown, but winter is over, and new life is coming. Spring is here, and the flowers are blooming, and you will reap everything you have sown in the battle—double portion—a hundredfold what the enemy has stolen."

9

Still Going
to the Other Side

Give ear to my prayer, O God,
And do not hide Yourself from my supplication.
Attend to me, and hear me;
I am restless in my complaint, and moan noisily…
- PSALM 55: 1-2 (NKJV)

As we closed the chapter on the tragedy, we began looking forward to the joy that was before us as October was fast approaching. However, about five days after the funeral, my husband began to feel sick. He started running a temperature and felt like he had the flu. We had been so careful at the funeral to follow all the COVID guidelines, and we had the dinner and funeral outside. But when he got tested, it came back positive.

I broke down and cried. I was scared for him and scared for me. I knew he was pretty healthy, but there was so much scary stuff on the news, and even though we had turned it all off, I had seen enough before we stopped watching to freak me out. If I got it, could my body fight it? I still wasn't 100% back to health and not yet eating normally.

We did what we were told to do: he isolated in our bedroom, and I slept on the couch. Luckily, we had a deck off our bedroom that connected to the back of the house where the kitchen was, so I could go out on the deck and visit with him, and he could get fresh air. He also had a bathroom in the master bedroom, and because he worked from home, if he chose to and was feeling like it, he could work from the bedroom.

I counted down the days of when they were saying symptoms would start. During this time, my dad also tested positive, and we found out a man from the funeral had tested positive. We deduced that they probably caught it at the dinner, even though it was outside, because they all used the same dipping utensils for the food.

A few days after my dad tested positive, my mom tested positive. I was very concerned now, because we had three family members with it simultaneously. My mom had a lot of pre-existing conditions that could make it deadly to older individuals. However, my dad was the one who was hit the hardest. I was dreadfully afraid we would lose him right after losing Jason's dad. I didn't think there was any way I would survive losing my dad.

COVID-19 QUARANTINE

We went through the quarantine period and I still had no symptoms. Jason was recovering quickly, and my mom seemed to do okay. We were still concerned about my dad and worried if Jason's mom might have gotten it; she also had pre-existing conditions and she was around Jason the day before he started showing symptoms. Miraculously, I never caught it from Jason or my parents.

We got COVID over and started preparing for the wedding. We were in charge of the rehearsal dinner, so I had to figure out food and decorations. I went through a roller coaster of emotions, from the fear that I would not be able to go to the wedding to the grief of one of my children moving out of my home, thus losing the ability to protect him all the time. And though I knew in my heart it was the right thing and he couldn't have found a more lovely and kind wife, it hurt a little to know someone else would be the one he would share his heart with, who would nurse him back to health when he was sick. It hurt that I wouldn't be seeing his face every day or know he was safe in his bed every night. I would miss our talks about theology and God. Hunter, my youngest, was always the one to have a smile on his face and give me a hug when I needed it and get me through anxiety that way, Michael was the one who was calm in a crisis and could talk me through and pray me through the attacks. A piece of my heart felt like it would be missing. So I went through the emotions that a mother goes through when she has a child leave her nest. I went through the nights of agonizing and pleading with God to please get me to the wedding. I kept my head in the promises He had given me and reminded myself that He had so much more ahead for me after this time. I reminded myself that we were still going to the other side of this fear and anxiety, and I was not quite there yet, so this was not over.

I started feeling bad emotionally and physically for a little while, feeling like I was slipping backwards once more. I couldn't understand after all the promises God had poured in, and after He had brought me through the funeral and opened up a new life for me, why now when the wedding was only weeks away, was I feeling bad again? I was disappointed because I thought my healing and freedom would look a certain way, and I put my timeline on God's promises. I believed I would get through the wedding with flying colors and eat the same thing at the wedding everyone else was. I believed that by the time it got here, I would be completely free. But God isn't on my timeline, and His promises are not on my timeline. Once the water breaks in labor, the labor process still has to occur. The labor process can take a few minutes, or it can take hours, but the mother doesn't get to quit in the middle because it isn't going the way she wanted it to go. She has to keep her eye on the joy that is to come and push through it. No matter how painful or how long it takes when she sees that baby, she will say it was all worth it.

The water has burst in my situation. Suddenly, the process of labor has begun, but the baby still hasn't been born. God hasn't yet birthed my promise. It hasn't happened the way I envisioned it would or in the timing I was hoping for, but I cannot give up in the middle of the process. It will be in God's perfect time and perfect way. It is not over yet. God isn't done. I will not count Him out or be disappointed. I will keep my eyes on the promise that is before me.

Though it is hard, I will allow myself to believe again and be excited again and expect again. God took me to Luke 5, where He told Peter to put out the nets one more time, and Peter said, *"We have been fishing all night and caught nothing, but because you said to, we will do it again."* I feel like that is where I was. God was telling me to put out my faith one more time and believe. And though I didn't want to because it would hurt again if I was disappointed, because He said to, I would do it.

After they obeyed and put out their nets, they took in more fish than they could even fit in their boats. Just because another storm came up in the middle of my journey to the other side doesn't mean the promises have changed. Now we are on our way once again, and I will not go back or jump out of the boat.

We are going to the other side!

Each battle the Israelites faced on the way to their promised land strengthened them. In the midst of it, they saw Who God was, and they saw Him fight for them and come through each time. By the time they made it to the promised land, those who remained could sustain what God had given them. They could trust God in new ways. In the battles and moments of intensity, the leaders emerged, and it was in the battles they found out who would stay faithful to God and who would turn aside to worship idols.

In the middle of the storm, on the way to the other side of the lake, the disciples saw Jesus. They saw Who He was and His power and authority to calm the storm (Mark 4:35-41). Even the *storm* was a part of the journey.

GOD SPEAKS

God spoke to me during this time, "All My promises still stand. Just because you haven't seen them yet, doesn't mean they are not coming. I do not lie. I am not a man that I should lie. I said it will happen, it will happen. Count it as done the moment I speak it forth. I am always faithful. I cannot go against My character. I am not that mean or harsh. I will not give you a promise and then take it away. I do not dangle good things in front of you and then snatch them back. Do not let your disappointment tell you I am not good. That is the voice of the enemy.

"All My words prove true. All My promises prove faithful. I will not change, and I cannot be shaken. My promises and My character are unshakable. It is steady and firm. If I promised it, you can take it to the bank. If you haven't seen it yet, then I am not done yet.

"Your circumstances do not change My promises. Do not put your eyes on a timeline or imagine the way it will happen. My timing and My ways are perfect and higher than yours. I know what I am doing. I see things you don't see and know things you don't know and perceive things you don't perceive.

"Keep your eyes fixed on the promise ahead, not on what is surrounding you now or what your feelings and emotions are telling you should happen, or it should look like. I know what I am doing. Trust Me. I know how to bring this about in a way that is absolutely best for you and will bring Myself glory and change lives around you. Trust Me. I love you.

"Proclaim My promises, speak them out, not what your thoughts or the enemy or your feelings and circumstances tell you. What I speak to you is the only truth that stands. Everything else is a lie. Again, I cannot and will never lie to you. I will never make you a promise and tell you I will do something and not see it through. As you know, it may not be when you want it or how you want it, but I will always fulfill My promises. Therefore, you have to trust Me completely and wholeheartedly, no matter what you see or feel.

"I am more real than those things. Those things can and will be shaken and change constantly. I am constant and steady, a firm foundation to plant your feet on, and because I am, My words are too.

"Stay the course. Don't let your disappointment cloud your vision and take you off the path. The path will lead you right where you need to be. The path leads home. It leads to the promised land where all the things I have spoken will be fulfilled. It is a land flowing with milk and honey. A land of freedom and healing and rejoicing.

"Stay on the path. The enemy will try to distract you but stay on the path to a new life like you have never lived before. A life full of joy and abundance until it overflows on those around you.

"Stay the course. You will get there. Just keep your eyes fixed on Me. I love you, my daughter. You are My prized possession, the apple of My eye, My baby girl. I want you whole, healed, and free. It is My will and plan for you. Just hold tight to Me and enjoy the journey home to freedom."

10

The Wedding
and the Virus

As for me, I will call upon God,
And the Lord shall save me.
- PSALM 55:16 (NKJV)

On October 26th, 2020, I wrote this in my journal:

God did it!!! I went to the wedding. He is so faithful! It
was God from beginning to end! Thank You, Jesus!

I made it through a funeral *and* a wedding and things were
looking up. I just *knew* this was the last stretch, and at any
moment, I was going to be completely healed and free. It was all
about to be fulfilled and complete. I was hoping the wedding
would be the moment that it would all happen, but it wasn't. Still,

that was okay because, at the moment, all I knew was I had made it to my son's wedding and was even able to walk down the aisle with him! My God was so faithful and so good!

It had been a true victory. At the rehearsal dinner I had been able to get up and speak. I made it through meeting all my new daughter-in-law's family, and both my boys and my husband were so proud of me. My boys said they felt like they were dreaming seeing me there. It felt so good, and just like the funeral, I can't tell you how it happened. I also can't tell you there was no anxiety before the wedding, but I can tell you that God showed up.

On the way to the wedding, I reminded myself He wasn't done, and we were not yet to the other side. That meant it was not over. But I could breathe a little easier now…

Or so I thought. The first week of November, my youngest son called to tell us he was sick. He had to be tested for COVID, and he came back positive. He had to leave college to come home and be quarantined. Since my husband had already had the virus, I let him take care of my son. Four days later, my worst fear happened, I began to get a sore throat.

I kept saying to myself, "it's just allergies or acid reflux," trying to assure myself that I would be okay. I also did my best to ignore the symptoms. The symptoms began the same day my son and his new wife came home from their honeymoon. At midnight, I awoke with a fever and I just began crying, telling my husband I didn't want to die. I tested positive, and we prepared for my son and me to both be isolated. We had everything we needed delivered to the house. Since my husband already had COVID, he took care of us both, and we let our son come out of his room and join us. I had remembered reading that it can take a turn for the worst after the fifth day, and if you make it to day eight, you are probably going to be okay. I counted days and hours. I went from reminding myself of God's promises to thinking maybe I had made all the promises up myself and I had nothing to stand on.

My symptoms never developed to anything serious, mainly a head cold and fatigue, so by the eighth day, I figured I would be okay. Then the fatigue hit me hard and I felt much the way I did when I had the virus back in 2017. I was tired and weak all the time. I cried and cried and told my husband I can't go through this for another two or three years. He reassured me that I was stronger than I was before and that this was just part of the virus. He told me that I would be back to normal before long, and he was right. After about a month of fatigue, my body began bouncing back.

In hindsight, God was so gracious not to let me get the virus when my husband got it, because that would have prevented me from attending the wedding. Thank You again, Jesus!

So, then we were in the Holiday Season, getting my strength back and leaving the virus behind. As I looked back on the whirlwind our lives had been since my father-in-law got sick at the beginning of September, and all the sustaining promises that God poured in all the way back in August, I cannot help but stand in awe of His care and love for me.

I remember writing in my journal that God gave me promises of healing and freedom, but there was a specific day before my father-in-law got sick that I wrote it would be a bumpy ride and that I would need to hold on tight to Him. How gracious He was to warn me. I am so grateful for my Father. I looked back and tried to figure out how I made it through all of that when just four months ago, I couldn't leave my house or be around anyone, or even walk very far. And now I have been through a funeral, a wedding, and COVID twice. The only answer I can come up with is **God showed up**. It was Him from beginning to end, and His goodness and faithfulness were not over yet!

December 17th, 2020

I feel like God is saying that this battle we have been in for the past 19 years has been a training ground preparing us for what we are about to step into. That He knew the timing all along, and we are about to step into what we were created for. This battle has strengthened our marriage and us individually. God knew what He was doing all along, even with Jason and I being put together. Everything has been in His hands all along.

We are about to see Him come through in ways we couldn't imagine, and things we haven't understood will make sense. I think of David and how God prepared him out in the pasture with the lion and the bear to defeat Goliath and then step into the palace as king.

Isaiah 43:1-2, 16-19 NLT "But now, O Jacob, listen to the Lord who created you. O Israel, the One who formed you, says, 'Do not be afraid, for I have ransomed you. I have called you by name; you are Mine. When you go through deep waters, I will be with you. When you go through rivers of difficulty, you will not drown. When you walk through the fire of oppression, you will not be burned up; the flames will not consume you. I am the Lord, who opened a way through the waters, making a dry path through the sea. I called forth the mighty army of Egypt with all its chariots and horses.

I drew them beneath the waves, and they drowned, their lives snuffed out like a smoldering candlewick. But forget all that—it is nothing compared to what I am going to do. For I am about to do something new. See, I have already begun! Do you not see it? I will make a pathway through the wilderness. I will create rivers in the dry wasteland.'"

December 24th, 2020

God is going to use my life as a beacon of hope and light, a testimony of His greatness, love, and power, His faithfulness to keep His promises. It hasn't happened in the time or way I hoped, but every moment had a purpose. It is all part of the story, and I will share it with others.

He is still a miracle-working God, and I feel like He is saying He is doing and about to do a miracle in my life, and my life will be the testimony to my family, that God is real, and He still does miracles, and He loves us. Not just to my family, but to everyone who knows or will hear my story. It will be a light of hope and healing.

I have fought a long and hard battle with anxiety and fear, but I have stayed the course and not given up. Now I will rest in the fulfillment of His promises in my life. I have sown tears and heartache, but it is time to reap the harvest of my tears.

Those tears watered the ground for my victory to grow. Instead of sadness and sorrow, I will see joy and peace. Instead of anxiety and fear, there will be calm and laughter. Beauty for ashes. Wings instead of chains. Soaring instead of falling. Rejoicing instead of mourning.

Leaping and jumping.

Victory instead of defeat. My time of breakthrough is here; my time of complete healing and deliverance has arrived.

"Believe it, just believe it! Begin rejoicing in it now. Celebrate it now. All the promises I have given you are about to see fulfillment. Get ready, get ready to tell your story. Get ready to shine brightly for My kingdom. The world lies in darkness, but a light has shown upon you. Jesus will shine through you."

Isaiah 60:1-2 NLT "Arise, Jerusalem! Let your light shine for all to see. For the glory of the Lord rises to shine on you. Darkness as black as night covers all the nations of the earth, but the glory of the Lord rises and appears over you."

Psalms 40:1-3 TPT "I waited and waited and waited some more, patiently, knowing God would come through for me. Then, at last, He bent down and listened to my cry. He stooped down to lift me out of danger from the desolate pit I was in, out of the muddy mess I had fallen into.

Now He's lifted me up into a firm, secure place and steadied me while I walk along His ascending path.

A new song for a new day rises up in me every time I think about how He breaks through for me! Ecstatic praise pours out of my mouth until everyone hears how God has set me free. Many will see His miracles; they'll stand in awe of God and fall in love with Him!"

11

He is Not Done

Cast your burden on the Lord,
And He shall sustain you;
He shall never permit the righteous to be moved.
- PSALM 55:22 (NKJV)

Welcome to 2021! Just when I thought everything was about to settle down, the whirlwind began again.

My husband and I had been talking about selling our home after our two boys moved out. Now one was married and one in college and no longer living with us, so we decided this was the right time. We had heard that the market was at a good place to sell, so on the 4th of January 2021, I called our realtor to see what she thought we could sell for. Little did I know she would tell me that we could sell the house that day if we really wanted to because she had a couple who needed a house and couldn't find one in the school district we lived in. We still had quite a bit of work to do on the house to get it ready to sell because we really didn't think we would be selling until March. She told us how much we could sell for and what we would profit, and it was enough that we knew we had to sell right then if we could. We got busy scrubbing and fixing everything we could because the couple was coming to look at the house the next weekend. Thank goodness my parents lived close because they were able to help us out, and by God's goodness, my uncle and aunt were visiting them, so they were able to help also. With all hands-on deck, we got everything done in time to show the house to the couple the next Sunday afternoon, the 10th of January.

At the same time, we were looking for new houses for ourselves. We looked at a couple, but they weren't in a good area or would need more work than we wanted to put in. Next, we expanded our search to an area we really didn't think we wanted to go to, but I found a house that had just come on the market that we decided to see the very next day. Our realtor told us they were already booked up with showings, so we would have only a small window of time to go in. We looked at the house and I knew almost immediately it was what I wanted. We were looking to downsize the house and get more land. This was exactly that. I wouldn't even have to paint anything. I didn't say anything to my husband until he came to a conclusion on his own. He was looking for particular things in the land. When we left the house, we agreed we both loved it and felt like it was the one we were meant to have. We called our realtor and told her to put in an offer for us. We knew it was a long shot because the other couple had not looked at our house yet, and it was not on the market yet, so we were putting in an offer contingent on the sale of our house without it even on the market. We both felt it was what God wanted us to do and we put the result in His hands.

Our realtor told us there were several offers on the home, and we would be last on the list because of the contingency. Because of this, we started looking again, just in case. We heard back that they accepted another offer before the weekend began. On Sunday, the couple came to see our home and they put in an offer immediately. Then things got really crazy.

My husband's biggest fear was that we would not find a house to live in. I asked my realtor on Monday if she could contact the realtor on the house one more time to see if the offer had gone through. She contacted me back and said there was some trouble with the offer, and if we put in a new offer for full price, contingent this time only on our house closing, they would accept it right away. I was absolutely ecstatic and overwhelmed. I told Jason that I knew it was the house for us and that God was working it all out. The couple buying our house began their inspections on that Tuesday. The inspection came back saying we needed a new roof due to hail damage, which we had no clue about, because who gets up on their roof and inspects it if it isn't leaking? Then there were some cracks they were worried about in the basement. My mind was whirling, and fear was trying to really take over. I cried because I was so afraid that it would fall through, and we would not get our house sold or be able to get the house we wanted to buy.

We called our insurance company about the roof to see if they would cover it. They sent out an inspector and said it would be covered! It also turned out we had Radon in our basement, which meant we had to take care of that before closing. I just was a mess, but I kept thinking to myself, why would God bring us this far in this deal and give us the house we wanted, and the couple buying our house really wanted it too, and everything was just falling into place, so why would He bring us to this point and let it all fall apart?

I can't say that I did not worry or wonder if it would all work out, but again, I had that glimmer of hope. In the end, everything worked out smoothly. We look back and absolutely see God's hands in the whole thing. Mostly we see the miracle of the fact that I was able to sell and buy a house and deal with realtors, and loan officers, and inspectors and cleaning and fixing the house, because a few months earlier, I would not have been. Still, once again, God did a miracle in me, and He came through with flying colors and blew my mind!

I was absolutely exhausted after we moved in and needed a lot of rest. God made sure I rested because right after we moved, we were snowed-in for five days, and my body was thankful for the rest. By this time, I was going into grocery stores and home stores and pretty much everywhere we needed to go. However, there was still one place that I had not set my foot in...

Resurrection Sunday

⁶ He is not here; for He is risen, as He said.
- MATTHEW 28:6 (NKJV)

By Resurrection Sunday, we were still settling into our new home. We had a new puppy and another one we were planning to get later in the year. We had five Nigerian Dwarf Goats. My husband, my dad, and my uncle were building fences and putting in flooring, and we were just very busy. In the midst of it all, I was pretty tired and honestly didn't get a lot of prayer time.

A couple of times, I paid for not resting as much as I should, and my body was beginning to feel it. I did not ask my husband for help with the animals because I knew he was tired from all he had to do, and I was the one that told him if he got me the goats and the puppy, I would take care of them. I was bottle feeding five baby goats every day, and when we first brought them home, they had to stay in the house because it was too cold for them to regulate their body temperatures. That meant I was cleaning up puppy pads and goat pens. At the same time, I was unpacking boxes and figuring out where everything needed to go. This was a task after going from a 3400-square-foot house with four bedrooms and four bathrooms and lots and lots of storage to an 1800-square-foot house. Thank God we had a three-car garage.

Baby goats – precious, adorable, and a lot of work.

As my body weakened, I got tired. I could feel the anxiety and depression wanting to set in again, and I began to get scared that I would fall back into the cycle. At one point, my husband told me I had to let him help me. He said he was waiting for me to ask for help, but when he figured out that I was not going to, he decided would *make me* let him help me. I am so grateful every day that God knew exactly who I would need to walk this journey with me. He knew who would be able to stand with me and not crumble, though I'm not saying there weren't days that he didn't want to. At this point, I had no choice but to let him help me, or I knew I would be back in a bad place again, and this time it would be because I was too stubborn to ask for help.

God began to speak to me that this home and the animals He had given me were going to be part of my healing. He told me that I need to enjoy the gifts He has given me. Enjoy my family and rest. He spoke to me that when the time comes that He launches me into His calling for me, this place will be a sanctuary for me, a place I can come back to and have rest and peace. He spoke to me about being a sponge, soaking up His presence and the things He would speak to me and show me. He wanted me to pursue Him. He gave me the example of how when you marinate meat, how it begins to take on the flavor of whatever you are marinating it in. As it marinates, it soaks up all that flavor and begins to taste like it. He said that is what He wants me to do with His presence. He told me that I was dry because I had not been soaking up His presence. And I was tired because I had been trying to do everything in my own strength.

Making Time for GOD

As much as I could with a new puppy and five baby goats, I began to try to spend time with Him again. It was hit and miss, and I knew I needed more, but I also knew His grace was with me. This time though, it wasn't because I thought I needed to do something to get Him to heal me. This time, He was speaking to me that I would need to spend time with Him because of where He was calling me to and what He wanted me to do. He was speaking to me that He wanted me to share my story and be a beacon of hope and healing to others who are where I have been. My story will be a testimony of God's love, grace, goodness, mercy, and power to my family and all who have watched my story unfold.

Now it is April, and Easter Sunday is here. I thought Saturday night about going to church but had talked myself out of it by bedtime. I was still a little wary of COVID and wasn't sure I wanted to be inside a building with so many people. I mainly knew Easter Sunday would be packed because that is one of the days that everyone goes to church, right? However, when I woke up Sunday morning, I saw that one of the churches I had watched online was having an outdoor service. I thought, hey, I could do an outside service, which would take some pressure off. I admit I was nervous, and I had to keep getting myself dressed even when the anxiety was yelling at me not to go. This time, the anxiety wasn't as loud. My body was so much stronger, and God had healed so much of my body, mind, and emotions that it didn't overtake me.

We went, and Easter Sunday 2021 was indeed my Resurrection Sunday! I get tears just thinking about it now. How good my God is that He would make me able to go to church for the first time in a little over seven years on Easter Sunday! It was overwhelming and so awesome to be there.

The following week I was also able to see my doctor and an allergist. I had not been to my doctor in over three years, and though she wanted me to see an allergist to try to figure out the food issues because by now, I was trying new foods, but reacting to everything, I couldn't go because of the fear and anxiety, until now. I also got an eye exam, which I needed for a very long time. I went to the salon and got a haircut, which I had not done in about ten years or more! God had broken through all my fears! He had set me free.

In this time, I was able to get answers about my food issues. The doctor did several allergy tests and tests for histamine problems. We figured out I may be having a histamine intolerance problem because of prolonged stress and anxiety. My gut was probably messed up because of having such a restricted diet for almost twenty years now. The allergist said to make sure I was not getting overly stressed and to start introducing new foods a tiny bit at a time, one at a time, until we could build the good bacteria back in my gut.

I am still believing for complete healing in my body, but things get better each day. Instead of two to three foods, now I am able to eat about ten different foods or more. God is so good and so faithful! Do I still have anxiety and fear? Yes, I am a human being living in a scary world, but it no longer paralyzes me and leaves me in a prison. I am free! It is for freedom Christ has set me free! I have to make sure I spend time with my Father, and I have to make sure I take time to rest my body and mind; those things are my responsibility. I know that my God showed up in my life. He showed up in a big way, and I stand in absolute awe of Him every single day of my life. I fall on my face, grateful to Him. I cannot stand in a worship service at church without tears running down my face when I think of His goodness and faithfulness to me! He is absolutely still in the miracle business.

Yes, I showed up, and I kept my heart toward Him, but I also doubted, and I questioned, and I didn't do all the things I was "supposed" to do, according to what I had been taught, and He still showed up and did a miracle in my life. Why? Because it is all about Him. His mercy. His grace. His love. His stripes. His death. His sacrifice. His Resurrection. His power. His ability. His strength. His finished work on a cross, not about me or you and what we can do!

It is Finished

For You are my hope, O Lord God;
You are my trust from my youth.
- PSALM 71:5 (NKJV)

One book does not have enough pages to describe our God. He is magnificent and gracious and loving and faithful and good, and so much more. If you are living with fear and anxiety, please hear me when I say this, THERE IS HOPE!!

It isn't about you doing more or being a better person or a better Christian. You have not failed! Your body needs rest. Your mind needs rest. Maybe you need help healing from some traumas and wounds in your life, but you, my dear one, are loved. You are precious. You are chosen. You are a royal priesthood. You are a masterpiece, knit together by the Creator's hands for a time such as this.

There is a plan and a purpose for your life. This is not the end. The fear and anxiety do not get to win. Jesus has overcome, and because of that, you will overcome. It is not about you and what you can or cannot do. It is not about you being strong enough or not having enough faith.

You are strong and courageous, and your heart is toward your God, or you would not have read this far in this book. Because of that, healing is yours. Freedom is yours! If you don't know Jesus, and He isn't the Savior of your soul, ask Him to be. Simply confess your sins and ask forgiveness and He will hear you and answer your prayer. You don't have to be in a church building or at an altar. You may be in your bedroom, in a hotel room, in a bar; it doesn't matter. He hears you, and He will answer you, and He will heal you.

Stop trying to work to get His love and affection. He already loves you *extravagantly*. He gave all He had for you. He wants to take you in His arms and comfort you and heal you as His child. He is your Father. A good, compassionate Father.

Psalms 103:3-14 (NLT): "He forgives all my sins and heals all my diseases. He redeems me from death and crowns me with love and tender mercies. He fills my life with good things. My youth is renewed like the eagle's the Lord gives righteousness and justice to all who are treated unfairly. He revealed His character to Moses and His deeds to the people of Israel. The Lord is compassionate and merciful, slow to get angry, and filled with unfailing love. He will not constantly accuse us, nor remain angry forever. He does not punish us for all our sins; He does not deal harshly with us, as we deserve. For His unfailing love toward those who fear Him is as great as the height of the heavens above the earth. He has removed our sins as far from us as the east is from the west. The Lord is like a father to His children, tender and compassionate to those who fear Him. For He knows how weak we are; He remembers we are only dust."

He will never abandon you or forsake you. He watches over you day and night. He never sleeps but keeps His eyes on you. He is your protector. He doesn't need you to be perfect because Jesus was perfect, and Jesus took our place.

Oh, dear friend, I want you to experience what I have experienced, where you can say with me as Job said, "I had only heard about you before, but now I have seen you with my own eyes." (Job 42:5 NLT)

You don't need to jump through hoops, just rest. Just let Him love you. Allow Him to heal you. Jesus has finished the work. It has nothing to do with you and everything to do with Him. Keep your eyes fixed on Him. Behold the cross, my friend! It is the turning point. Everything hinges and pivots on that one point. Keep your eyes there and know that no matter what you have been taught you have to do, no matter who told you that you won't make it, no matter who told you that you are not good enough, pretty enough, smart enough, no matter who says it cannot be done, you will never be healed, God says, IT IS FINISHED!!

Love like I have never known has pierced my heart and healed my soul. A Father so good and true has done what I couldn't do. He picked me up out of the pit and set my feet on solid ground. He saved my soul that once was lost but now is found. He healed my wounds with His tender touch. He whispers to me, *I love you so much.* Love so true and so pure, I don't deserve a love so sure. But He washed me clean, removed my guilt and shame, because of His sacrifice, I will never be the same.

Photo Album

My boys – never shy in front of the camera!

Bringing Luna home.

Max & Luna

Hunter and Abbey engagement.

Michael and Jenna engagement.

Jason, me, Michael, Jenna, and Hunter at Michael's wedding.

Finally, a few "just because" fun family Christmas pics.

Acknowledgments

I want to thank, first and foremost, My Father, who never let go of me through it all. Without His breath, His strength, and His love, I would not be here today. Jesus Christ, for being the sacrifice for me so that I could live.

I want to thank my husband, Jason. I couldn't have gotten through this without you; you are my hero. You are my best friend, my shoulder to cry on, and my rock. I love you more than words can say. You have spoken the truth over me even when I didn't want to hear it. You were my voice when I couldn't speak. You were in the trenches with me every moment.

My boys, Michael and Hunter, you are my gifts from God. You made me laugh when I didn't think I could smile again. You sat and talked with me. Your smiles, your prayers, your hugs helped me heal. You gave me strength and reason to keep going every day. I miss your faces at home. I love you both to the moon and back.

My parents, you are my cheerleaders. You sacrificed so many times to come to stay with me so that I wouldn't have to be alone. You have cried with me and prayed with me. I am thankful to have you on my side. I love you both dearly.

Thanks also to my brother, Robert, for always making me laugh in the bad times. And those beautiful nieces of mine, Star and Lauren. You both have shown me what true courage is in the midst of bad situations.

To my daughter-in-law, Jenna thank you for always being encouraging and supportive.

To my future daughter-in-law, Abbey, thank you for being so kind and for being willing to take the pictures for the book cover.

Many family members, including my in-laws, always supported me, prayed for me, and loved me well. Robert Murray, you will always be remembered well. I know you are in heaven rejoicing with me. So many other family members also prayed and encouraged and supported me, and I will never forget it. I love you all forever.

Janela Meacham, God connected us seven years ago for a reason. You have become a best friend, a prayer partner, and a confidant. There were days I know without your one text asking me how I was, and knowing I could be truthful with you and that you didn't just want to hear, "I am okay", I would not have made it. Thank you, my friend. I love you dearly.

Kitty Martin, thank you for never compromising, even if you thought I wouldn't want to hear it. Thank you for all the messages and encouragement. You have cheered with me, grieved with me, and prayed for me. You are my mentor and my friend. We are on this journey entwined together, and I will never forget you. Love you dearly.

And thank you to Ellen Sallas, my editor and assistant publisher, and now friend. Ellen has encouraged me and cheered me on throughout the process of getting this book ready. She has given me creative wings. I have no doubt ours was a divine connection.